CW01368931

The Cult of the Green Bird

The Cult of the Green Bird

*The Mythology of the
Green Woodpecker*

Antony Clare Lees

Copyright © Antony Clare Lees, 2002

First published in 2002 on behalf of the author
by Scotforth Books,
Carnegie House,
Chatsworth Road,
Lancaster LA1 4SL,
England
Tel: +44(0)1524 840111
Fax: +44(0)1524 840222
email: carnegie@provider.co.uk
Publishing and book sales: www.carnegiepub.co.uk
Book production: www.wooof.net

All rights reserved.
Unauthorised duplication
contravenes existing laws.

British Library Cataloguing-in-Publication data
A catalogue record for this book is available from the British Library

ISBN 1-904244-13-0

Typeset in Adobe Garamond by Carnegie Publishing

Printed and bound in the UK by
The Cromwell Press, Wiltshire

*To Joanna
who shared in this quest*

Fortunatus et ille deos qui novit agrestis
And happy he who knows the rustic gods.

(Virgil, *Georgics, ii*)

Contents

Illustrations ix
Acknowledgements x

Introduction 1

The Woodpecker King 11

Leader of the Tribe 23

Rome – the Bird of Mars 28

Messengers of the Gods 43
           Divination 43
           Oracles 52

The Rain Bird 56

The Legend of the Springwort 67

Picus and the Plough 78

The Bee-Wolf 83

The Woodpecker in Literature 88

Bestiaries and Emblems 95

Conclusion 98

Folk Names of the Green Woodpecker	109
Bibliography	112
Index	115

Illustrations

1 The Green Woodpecker   6
2 The William Morris Tapestry   36
3 A ring from the Thetford Treasure   40
4 An intaglio, first or second century BC   53
5 Ringstone, probably Italian, first
   century BC   55
6 Carved woodpeckers on a bench-end,
   sixteenth century   101

Acknowledgements

I am indebted to the author, Wilfred Willett and Messrs. A. & C. Black for permission to quote from a passage in *British Birds*, published in 1948; also to HarperCollins Publishers Ltd for permission to quote from Gilbert Murray's Introduction to his translation of Aristophanes' 'The Birds', originally published by Allen & Unwin Ltd in 1950.

Introduction

SOME BIRDS HAVE ALWAYS APPEALED to man's imagination more than others; the strength and majestic flight of the eagle, the soft beauty of the dove and the song of the nightingale have all been admired and incorporated into early mythology and culture. The subject of this book, the green woodpecker, would seem to have had a particular fascination for man since the earliest times. This is not a bird which haunts the abodes of mankind, but when seen it is not to be ignored. A sudden glimpse of its brilliant green and yellow plumage and scarlet head will make even the most disinterested observer look again, and anyone who spends time in the countryside of southern Britain and many parts of Europe will become aware of this bird, even if they do not know its name.

The green woodpecker has all the qualities required of a bird of omens and portents. It is common enough to be familiar but rare enough never to be taken for granted. Come across one in the fields or at the edge of a wood and its behaviour cannot be predicted in advance; each bird is an individual. It may depart, showing its yellow rump as it goes, with a distinctive undulating flight; another time it may merely fly on to a nearby tree: to the casual eye it is no longer visible and appears to have flown on, but often this is not so. If you stand still when this has happened and keep a watch on the tree you may well see a head and one bright eye. The woodpecker has put the trunk or a branch between itself and the intruder and is peering round from time to time to observe you.

Then there is the call, which may be heard at any time of the year and again there is uncertainty and a lack of predictability. The familiar songbirds of our countryside can be heard all day in springtime, although later in the year they fall silent and it would be difficult to envisage a blackbird or thrush as an oracular bird or even a weather prophet; their songs are a much-loved background sound among our fields and hedgerows but they do not stand out. It is not so with the green woodpecker. His call is unmistakable but full of variations; Gilbert White in his *Natural History of Selborne* described it as 'a sort of loud and hearty laugh'. It is made with the head thrown back and coming from a position well up in a tree can be heard from a great distance. The name of 'yaffle', often given to the bird is an imitation of its call, while in Gloucestershire it was known as Laughing Betsy. The length of the 'laugh' seems to vary with the individual bird but when surprised its alarm note is usually short and querulous, although when approached by a sparrow hawk it may be longer, with a high-pitched hysterical sound. It is also reliably recorded as drumming occasionally, using its bill on a branch which acts as a sounding board; however this is unusual and when heard is a weaker performance than that habitually given by the great spotted species.

To the ornithologist the subject of this study is *Picus viridis*, one species amongst a large family of woodpeckers, which is placed among the Piciformes, the second most evolved of the twenty-seven orders, or major groups, of birds. Piciformes includes such diversified families as toucans and barbets. The family of woodpeckers, which includes more than two hundred members, probably evolved their skills in the Eocene period, more than fifty million years ago and are specially adapted to obtain their food by drilling and probing within the bark of trees for grubs and insects. Their strong claws, two facing forward and two to the rear, are designed like climbing irons to grip the bark, while the stiff tail helps to brace the bird in a vertical position against the tree trunk. A powerful straight beak acts as a chisel, which is used to drill into a tree with a series of rapid blows, while a very long tongue, barbed at the tip, is used to seek out the woodpecker's prey. This 'tongue' is actually a highly specialized apparatus consisting of the hyoid, made of bone and elastic tissue, attached at one end to the actual tongue which is quite short; it then passes under the jaw and around the back of the head where it is anchored in the right nostril. When stretched this allows the tongue to protrude to a distance five times longer than the bird's beak and is ideal for picking up ants and delving into the galleries made by wood-boring insects and grubs in the timber.

The green woodpecker, unlike the other species found in Britain, spends much of its time on the ground seeking out ants' nests, which it probes with its long bill and then uses its tongue to pull out the pupae as well as the adult insects. The stab marks made by its beak are a familiar sight on ant hills and downland turf where a yaffle has been at work.

Breeding and roosting is in holes, hollowed out of tree trunks, which the birds bore out with their bills. A horizontal entrance, slightly elliptical and sloped to keep out the rain leads into a chamber descending vertically for twelve to fifteen inches, at the bottom of which a few wood chips are left as a lining to the nest. Most of the chips produced during the excavation are thrown out of the nest hole and the sight of these at the foot of a tree in spring is often an indication that a nest is being excavated; the entrance is usually orientated towards the north or east so that the heat of the noonday sun is avoided in the nest. The excavation of such a hole is a laborious task for any woodpecker but particularly so for the green, which being less specialized as a tree dweller, does not have such a powerful bill. Perhaps for this reason it is not uncommon for the green woodpecker to reuse a hole for nesting for a second season and afterwards for solitary roosting.

About half a dozen oval whitish eggs are laid, usually in May and incubation by both birds lasts for about eighteen days. After hatching, the young birds remain in the nest for about three weeks; food is brought by both parents in the form of a milky-white paste which is regurgitated by the adult birds into the gaping mouths of the youngsters. A pouch in the bird's oesophagus allows it to store a considerable quantity of food in this way, enough to produce about fifteen portions so that each fledgling can be fed several times during one visit to the nest. This means that, unlike the great spotted woodpecker which brings back food in its beak every ten or fifteen minutes, the green woodpecker only needs to return about once in three quarters of an hour, which is a considerable advantage, not only in saving time and effort but also in reducing the risk of predators locating the nest by observing the birds going to and fro. Nevertheless it is during this period that one is most likely to find a nest, having been led to it by a constant chorus of cries from the young birds, which can be heard from a considerable distance, rising to a crescendo when they hear the adult birds approaching with food.

As the young birds grow older and stronger it is often possible to see the head of one protruding from the entrance to the nest, as it looks out for the return of its parent. At this stage it is comical to hear the continuous raucous cries of the nestlings, occasionally punctuated by a precocious attempt at the laughing call of the adult bird. The instinct to peck vigorously with their bills is well developed in the young birds and when feeding them the parents can be seen to dodge out of the way of their lunging offspring and choose a safe moment to put the food into their mouths.

The Cult of the Green Bird

1. *The Green Woodpecker.*
Photograph: *Aquila Wildlife Images (S.C. Brown).*

The young birds are finally coaxed to leave the hole by the adult birds calling from nearby and having once made their first momentous flight from the nest, they do not return to it. Their parents continue to feed them for a few weeks after which they gradually become more independent. Their juvenile plumage, which gives a speckled appearance on the neck and breast, is lost during the first moult in August or September.

The green woodpecker does not frequent dense woodland but prefers comparatively open countryside or parkland with deciduous trees. These birds are very much individuals, both in habits and voice. Some seem to have a preference for a particular species of tree and I have noticed that one bird will make its way from one ash tree to another in mixed woodland, while another keeps almost exclusively to oak or beech.

The calls also are distinctive. There is, of course, always a difference between the full laughing call given mainly in the spring and the shorter alarm notes, but this apart, it is quite easy to distinguish individual birds by their calls which vary from rather harsh guttural versions to beautiful flute-like notes, the number of which in one call seeming to be standardized by each bird.

In Britain the green woodpecker is generally distributed in England and Wales but it is scarce in Scotland, although milder winters seem to be encouraging it to spread further north. It is not found in Ireland. It is not adapted to tolerate high altitudes or severe winters, since deep snow will prevent access to its food supply. Within these constraints however, it is found throughout Europe and South East Asia.

Two other species of woodpecker are sufficiently similar to the green woodpecker (*Picus viridis*) to be confused with it in folk tradition. The grey-headed woodpecker (*Picus canus*) looks rather like the green woodpecker, although somewhat smaller and with a grey head; the male only has red on the forehead but not on the crown. Its feeding habits are much the same as the yaffle's, as is the call, although this is not as full-throated and is only heard in the breeding season. Its territory overlaps that of the green woodpecker in parts of France, Germany and central Europe and it is found as far east as China. Levaillants green woodpecker (*Picus vaillantii*) may also be confused with *Picus viridis*, being very similar but lacking the red moustachial stripe which is a mark of the male green woodpecker. However it is only found in Africa along the Mediterranean shore in Morocco, Algeria and Tunis, frequenting groves of scattered oaks.

It is possible that on occasions the larger black woodpecker was the subject of some of the myths and legends which have been carried down to us. This bird also has a red head, which figures in many of the stories but it is shyer and much rarer than the green woodpecker, preferring coniferous forests at higher altitudes and it is perhaps mainly in Scandinavia that the black species was portrayed. However even in Norway, where the black woodpecker is reasonably common, confirmation of the unique status of the green bird comes from a traveller in that country writing in the late 19th century.* He records that people there considered the green woodpecker to be better than a barometer, predicting the weather three days ahead. A loud and monotonous call foretold fine weather, a low call, rain and storm approaching, but if the bird came near the house a tempest was to be expected! The author shot one of these birds and was nearly involved in some trouble. The peasants had a superstitious veneration for the green bird but, he relates, the black species was not venerated in this way.

The green woodpecker, with its bright colours and laughing call would have attracted more attention to itself. It also spends much more time on the ground than other woodpeckers and is therefore more likely to have been associated with man's first attempt at ploughing and sowing crops; there is also no doubt that it has always been considered to be the 'rain bird'.

The earliest reference to the bird which gives a hint of its involvement in mythology comes from Babylon where it was known as the Axe of Ishtar, goddess of fertility. From Greece there are many traditions regarding the god Picus (the woodpecker) and in Crete he was equated with Zeus himself. To the Romans, Picus was a god of the forests, a son of Saturn and a prophet who was turned into a woodpecker; this was also the bird of Mars, protector of Romulus and Remus and revered throughout Italy, where it was consulted by

---

* Lloyd, *Scandinavian Adventures*.

The Cult of the Green Bird

means of oracles and gave its name to one of the tribes occupying central Italy. It figures in folklore right across Europe as a weather prophet connected with thunder and rain and the magic herb, the springwort, is invariably associated with it.

Running through much of the mythology and later folklore related to the woodpecker there seems to be a theme which suggests a bird god, or at least a bird representing a god, which was later replaced by more anthropomorphic gods and later, of course, by Christianity. It is the object of this book to attempt to unravel the tangled threads of these tales which stretch back into prehistory.

The Woodpecker King

ARISTOPHANES IN HIS PLAY *The Birds*, which was first produced in Athens in the year 414 BC, refers to an old story that the Woodpecker once ruled until Zeus took the sceptre from him. The play is a comedy, but for such an allusion to make sense to his audience Aristophanes must have been confident that they would have been familiar with a tradition going back to a much earlier time and predating the pantheon of Greek gods and goddesses, but how did it arise?

Birds have been the neighbours of man throughout his sojourn on this planet since they have been here for a far longer time. The earliest fossil of a primitive bird, half reptile but with feathers, has been dated to one hundred and fifty million years ago. By the time *Homo sapiens*, our direct ancestor, was roaming the earth a mere quarter of a million years ago, bird species which we would recognize today had been around for two million years or so. Early man must have been very conscious of the birds around him, many brightly coloured, with their strange calls and fascinating variety of song and above all their power of flight into a realm which he could not enter. The sky has always seemed

The Cult of the Green Bird

to be the source of life-giving forces and higher powers; it was from above that the sun shone and the rain-bearing clouds appeared. Sometimes the lightning flashed and the thunder rolled, bringing not only the vital element of water but on occasion a natural and awe-inspiring manifestation of another great force – fire.

For all these things man looked upwards, and so it would be natural to 'look up' to birds as they rose above the tree tops of the primeval forest or soared effortlessly over the plains. They walked on two legs like himself and derived their sustenance from hunting and gathering as he did, and yet they had this magical power of flight which he lacked. Such creatures must have seemed at the very least to be messengers or symbols of those greater beings whose bounty man sought to invoke from above.

Birds as gods, or gods represented as birds, can be found as far back in our history as written records or surviving artifacts can take our knowledge. As we seek to penetrate the mists of prehistoric times it is hard to tell whether they were merely symbols used to depict gods and spirits or whether man really worshipped birds themselves. It is difficult to enter into the minds of our remote ancestors and misleading to judge their religious thought by the very few clues which have come down to us. If Christianity had been known to us only by its buildings and their furnishings without the benefit of an explanation through the written word, what a garbled and distorted picture would have been left to us. Our prehistoric ancestors could only hand down their beliefs

The Cult of the Green Bird

from generation to generation by word of mouth until they became crystallized into myths and it is in this form that they have reached us. Inevitably this has left us with some distortions; allegorical tales have come down to us as straightforward beliefs and bird or animal-shaped beings may be shamans' masks or represent certain spiritual facets, as in the gods of ancient Egypt.

Theories concerning the mental reasoning of early man are numerous and varied, some emphasizing the brutish nature of existence among the first hunter-gatherers who roamed the earth, desperately seeking to remain alive and perpetuate their kind in a hostile world in which fear of known and unknown perils encouraged a primitive magic, which sought to influence the odds stacked against them. Others prefer to emphasize man's divine nature and his natural attunement to higher influences, if not to a specific deity.

Perhaps it is not too difficult to reconcile both these ideas. Daily life must have been concentrated on sheer survival and an instinctive desire to obtain what help was possible from any source. At the same time the world must have been a very beautiful place and it would be foolish of us to suppose that primitive man was not moved by the beauty of the landscape, a flower or the night sky and did not feel himself part of a whole which was greater than himself.

The question of how man first turned to religion and indeed the very definition of that word has prompted long debates amongst scholars and occupied many volumes, and it would not be appropriate to enter into the subject in any depth here. However in the first place it is necessary to define the meaning of 'religion' which perhaps may be taken to be the recognition by man of a being or beings superior to himself. Most writers seem to agree that it entails an element of mystery but if the recognition is limited to a mere acceptance of the existence of supernatural powers, with no acknowledgement of higher beings it is considered by many anthropologists that this should only be described as magic. A magician attempts to manipulate the power for his own purposes and there is no element of prayer or supplication.

It is generally thought that an early stage was a belief in animism, a feeling that everything in nature, be it animal, stone or wood has life in it, or literally, breath. This rather vague concept crystallised into something more definite, a recognition of more specific powers centred on a particular area or thing. In the classical tradition these came to be known as numina. A numen has no exact English counterpart; literally it may be defined as 'that which is produced by nodding', implying a spirit with power of its own, capable of producing some effect with a mere nod, or as we might say 'without lifting a finger'. These numina were not gods and had no individual personalities but they came to be associated with certain places, perhaps groves or springs of water around which there was a special atmosphere where particular favours could be sought. The same concept is applied by anthropologists to 'mana', a Polynesian word covering the idea of most ancient peoples of the existence of any unseen mystical emanation, good or evil. It might be found in animals, a fortunate person, thunder, a volcano or even a stone which had caused a man to trip.

Clearly birds would have been seen to have mana but how could man gain their cooperation? Seeking an answer to this led to totemism, which in some guise or other seems to have been an almost universal stage in the development of religion and should probably be regarded as an intermediate step between the practice of magic and the recognition of specific gods. The word totem is sometimes used simply to describe a heraldic type of device taken by an individual or a group as a distinguishing mark or badge, but totemism in its full sense implies a deeply felt link between the totem and the group concerned. In recent history it can be found amongst the aboriginal tribes of Australia and is probably best known as part of the culture of the Red Indian tribes of North America. Amongst both of these, animals and birds figure as the principal totem objects.

A totem is not a god, although the creature concerned may well be regarded as the messenger of the god or gods. To a member of the Australian aboriginal Crow Tribe, 'Crow' is his elder brother, his soul mate. The bond is an intensely personal one and an extension of the close relationship one member of the tribe has with another and to the bird kingdom, which seemed perfectly natural to our ancestors. At the same time the totem is wiser than man, or rather is considered to have access to a wider knowledge.

The Cult of the Green Bird

But what of the woodpecker? The earliest reference to this bird in any religious context seems to be in the literature of ancient Babylon where it was known as the Axe of Ishtar and described as green. Ishtar was the goddess of love and fertility, associated with the planet Venus. Her consort was Tammuz, a male god, originally a tree god but later concerned with vegetation in general. The wedding of these two gods was celebrated annually as far back as the third millennium BC, at Uruk on the Euphrates.

Babylon was of course part of the fertile crescent in which agriculture was thought to have begun and it was the requirement for favourable weather conditions and skills in growing crops which brought the worship of an Earth Mother, a great goddess, to the fore. Such a concept travelled westward and it is in Crete that the next references to the woodpecker are found. Here the idea of an Earth Mother in partnership with a green god, born each spring and dying as the vegetation sank back in the autumn was well-established: her male partner was Zeus, and Crete has been credited with having both his place of birth and his grave. It was the Cretans' claim that Zeus was buried on their island which caused the Greeks on the mainland to say that the Cretans were great liars, since to their way of thinking the idea of an immortal god dying was absurd.

According to the traditional myth, Cronos, the youngest of the Titans who were the children of Uranus and Gaia, gods of Heaven and Earth respectively, always swallowed his new-born children out of jealousy. Rhea, his wife bore the infant Zeus secretly in a cave in Crete and gave Cronos a stone wrapped in swaddling clothes which he immediately swallowed. In case Cronos should hear the baby crying the Curetes danced around the cradle clashing their swords against their bronze shields; these were young men, half warriors, half priests, who seem to have originated as earth-spirits and came to be associated with the cult of Rhea.

Both the great mountain peaks of Crete, Ida and Dicte, were claimed to be the birth place of Zeus. In later times a compromise accepted Dicte as the actual place of birth but laid down that the god was educated by the Curetes on mount Ida. The cave at Dicte has been identified and excavated. It is a large double cavern, five hundred feet above the village of Psychro. A cult object found in the cave on Mount Ida is a large bronze shield of the 9th or 8th century BC; in its centre an athletic-looking god has one foot on a bull and is lifting a lion above his head, while winged attendants on each side seem to hark back to Assyrian themes. However it is clearly the youthful Zeus and the Curetes who are depicted. The woodpecker has been given only a minor role in the myths surrounding the birth and the story of Celeus (meaning green woodpecker) coming to steal the honey which was given to the infant god is discussed in another chapter.

Here in Crete the goddess's male partner was later known as Cretan Zeus to distinguish him from the Zeus of the mainland, who as overlord of the pantheon of the gods of Olympus was immortal. A number of

The Cult of the Green Bird

classical writers refer to his tomb but do not agree as to its location. Michael Psellus, writing in the 11th century, recorded that the legend was still alive and related that the people of Crete showed the grave with a cairn above it. Buondelmonti visited Mount Juktas in 1415 and described a cave by the road leading to it; in the upper end of the cave he was shown the grave of Zeus with an illegible inscription. In 1555 Belon says the tomb was still to be seen on the mountain of Sphagiotes and 19th century travellers told the same tale.

A somewhat confusing link with Picus is recorded in the context of this tomb by Suidas who relates that King Picus, having ruled over Eluisis, died at the age of 120 and left instructions that he was to be buried on the island of Crete with an inscription reading:

> Here lies dead Picus who is also Zeus.

The mythical kingdom of Picus has been variously located by different authors, going back to the 2nd century BC and the point of these myths seems to have been to explain the rise and fall of the first great empires of the world. Georgios Kedranos, who lived about AD 1100, collated these accounts and recorded Nebrod (i.e. Nimrod) as the first king on earth and founder of Babylon. Picus, who came to call himself Zeus, expelled Nimrod (or Cronos) from his kingdom and the latter fled to Italy and became ruler there. Later Picus quitted Babylon and took over from Cronos in Italy reigning there until he died and was buried in Crete.

The Minoan civilization which emerged in the bronze

age was peaceful and prosperous due to a flourishing maritime trade. The island was ruled by priest-kings, said to be descended from Minos, and the Great Goddess was worshipped in different guises; as well as being the Earth Mother she was Guardian of the Mountains, of Trees and Wild Beasts. She was often depicted with flowers, birds and beasts and most commonly with the sacred double axe, representing thunder. A.B. Cook* suggested that the axe was linked with the woodpecker which was known as the axe bird but there is no direct evidence of such a cult in Crete. What has survived in the mythology of mainland Greece is a persistent tradition which brought together Picus and Zeus, either as two names for one god-king who lay buried in Crete or as rivals for a throne to which Zeus succeeded in place of an earlier bird-king. Many of the stories seem contradictory but this is hardly surprising as myths evolved to account for historic events and changes in religious beliefs.

In some myths of the Greeks it is a human who is turned into a bird. Polytechnos (meaning craftsman) was said to be a carpenter who lived at Colophon in Lydia and he possessed an axe given to him by Hephaestus, the god of craftsmen. Polytechnos and his wife Aedon lived happily together until they let it be known that they thought they were more in love than Zeus and Hera. Angered by this piece of irreverence Hera despatched Discord to bring disharmony between

---

* Cook, A.B., *Zeus*.

the two mortals. Polytechnos was working on a chariot seat and Aedon was weaving a web of cloth. It was agreed that the one who finished first should receive the present of a slave girl from the other. Hera helped Aedon to finish first and Polytechnos, angry at being defeated, went to see Aedon's father and pretended that his wife had sent him to fetch her sister, Chelidon. On the way home Polytechnos raped the girl, cut off her hair, dressed her in strange clothes and, threatening to kill her if she revealed the truth, presented her to her sister as the promised slave. Eventually the over-worked Chelidon told Aedon the truth and the two sisters planned their revenge. Having tricked Polytechnos into eating the flesh of his own child they returned to their father's house pursued by the now distraught husband who was captured, bound and thrown amongst the sheep, smeared with honey to attract flies. Aedon, her anger turned to pity, tried to keep the flies off but her father and brother then wished to kill her as well. At this point Zeus feeling that enough was enough, stepped in and turned all the characters in the drama into birds. Pandareos, the father, became a sea-eagle, Aedon a nightingale, her brother a hoopoe and Chelidon a swallow. As for Polytechnos the carpenter, he became a woodpecker.

  This story, with features such as the father eating his child's flesh and the honey has some echoes of the tale of the birth of Zeus. In many of these myths men are

The Cult of the Green Bird turned into birds but this is really an inversion of what actually happened; the bird gods had been replaced by gods like men, with most of mankind's feelings and foibles.

Aristophanes' play shows that in earlier times birds had been venerated, if not actually worshipped, and the woodpecker was to the fore in this tradition. When the pantheon of gods was established on the Greek mainland, the older, simpler nature gods handed down through Cretan beliefs had to be fitted into the new order and the woodpecker myth split into several strands. Picus lost his regal powers to Zeus, who was then said to rule the sky and hence the weather, including thunder, his most awesome manifestation. Nevertheless the woodpecker was still felt to have 'mana', his magic power and his status as the rain bird and first ploughman was carried forward into folk belief. As a totem Picus gave his name to an Italian tribe which he led to a new land and his reputation as a prophet and soothsayer was used to good effect in divination. These facets are considered in more detail in later chapters. At times he seems to have become an appendage of Mars, an agricultural god worshipped by many tribes as such before he was considered to be a god of war. In another guise King Picus was fitted into the gods' family tree as the son of Saturn (equated with Cronos) and given a part in the founding of Rome.

Returning to Greece, an oracle in which the woodpecker figured is recorded (*Didot* III, 6), and Pan was said to have been born from a woodpecker's egg. The bird's powers have persisted in folk memory; according to J.C. Lawson in *Modern Greek Folklore and Ancient*

The Cult of the Green Bird

Greek Religion. The laugh of the woodpecker, owing to its mocking sound, was considered to be a sign that an intrigue against someone's person or pocket was in train. If the bird was seen or heard on one's right this was a good omen; crossing from left to right was also fortunate on the basis that all is well that ends well. If the woodpecker laughed on the right the hearer might proceed to cheat his neighbour with full confidence but if on the left he must be wary to baffle intrigues against himself! A single or twice repeated call was lucky but if heard three times it was a bad omen.

The Cult of the Green Bird

Leader of the Tribe

THE TRAIL OF THE WOODPECKER CULT next takes us across the Adriatic to the Italian Peninsula, where before the time of Rome the country was occupied by numerous small tribes, one of which actually took its name from the woodpecker. Strabo in his *Geography* tells us that the Piceni originally came from the land of the Sabines and that a woodpecker, regarded by them as sacred to Mars, led the way for them to their new land of Picenum which was named after this bird, known in their language as 'Picus'.

The migration of tribes in this way originated in the custom of the Sacred Spring (the Ver Sacrum), initially a religious rite used to avert some natural calamity or to ensure victory in battle. With such an end in view the tribal leaders would promise to dedicate everything born in the following spring to their god and this would of course include any children born at that time. The newly-born were not required to be sacrificed but were consecrated to the god to whom the vow had been made. On reaching adulthood they had perforce to leave their families and home territory and set out to find a new land in which to settle, led by a creature sacred to the god to whom they had been dedicated at birth. In this way, apart from the woodpecker, animals such as the bull and the wolf gave their names to tribes. The practice apparently continued down to historical times and was clearly a means of spreading out the population of a tribe which had become too concentrated in one area.

The Piceni settled in the area which in modern times is roughly covered by the central and southern portions of the Marches Region of Italy and the northern part of the Abruzzi. Strabo states that Picenum stretched from the River Esino to Castium, now Guilianova. If we accept Strabo's statement that the Piceni came from the land of the Sabines it can be assumed that among these peoples the woodpecker was held in esteem, otherwise it would not have been chosen as the totem for the offshoot of the tribe which migrated to Picenum. The origins of the many different peoples who occupied the Italian peninsula are disputed by historians. Some regard the Picenti as descendants of the original Neolithic people but others consider that they were invaders from Illyria who mingled with the indigenous population. Their language, as recorded later, was Indo-European and similar to Illyrium, and if Illyria was indeed their place of origin it would account for the woodpecker's cult crossing the Adriatic.

The picture of them which has come down to us from the archaeological finds of stelae and weapons is of a warlike people who traded widely and fought against the pirates of the Adriatic at sea. The Picentes' relations with Rome as the latter became dominant throughout Italy was also turbulent. In 299 BC Rome hurriedly formed an alliance with the Picentes against the Gauls who had crossed the Alps and were advancing towards Rome. Some thirty years later it was the Picentes who rebelled against the Romans. Suppressed by the might of the legions they were incorporated into the Roman fold as 'cives sine suffragio', half-citizens, and at the same time a Latin colony was founded at Firnum to oversee them.

Rome now had a firm grip on most of the peninsula; the degree of independence retained by the various tribes was determined by their previous behaviour. Some were nominally allies of Rome, others had full or half citizenship under Roman rule. The forms of government varied, with many peoples retaining considerable control over their own local affairs, but true sovereignty lay at the centre and tribute by taxes and military service was required from all. In 241 BC the Picentes were rewarded for their loyalty during the wars with Carthage with full citizenship; at the same time they were given access to the *Comitia Centuriata*, an early legislative assembly. This was divided on tribal lines and two new tribes were created at this time, one being for the Picentes. The system had the advantage of maintaining tribal links in the Assembly but soon afterwards the number of tribes was fixed at a total of thirty-five and thereafter as fresh people were enfranchized they were distributed at random amongst the tribal groups in the Assembly. Thus began the breakdown of regional distinctions and the distinctions between individual tribes gradually became blurred.

In Italy the woodpecker became associated with Mars, a god who seems to have been generally worshipped among the tribes who invaded the peninsula from the north. Mars was an agricultural god, concerned with the fertility of crops and animals and only later becoming associated with war. Assuming that Picus was brought in by the newcomers from the other side of the Adriatic where they would have been in proximity to Greek culture, it is easy to imagine how the ambivalent status, which is revealed in later Roman times, came about. At that stage Picus retained his own identity as a minor god or early king and at the same time had become the bird of Mars. This is what we would expect if the cult of the woodpecker was superimposed on to the traditions of the earlier settlers who would have found that Picus held sway over much the same facets of their beliefs as Mars.

Written evidence of religious customs in Italy before the Romans is of course extremely rare, but at Gubbio, the ancient city of Iguvium, several bronze tablets have been preserved. The earliest date from 400/300 BC, written in the Umbrian dialect while the latest date from 80 BC using the Latin alphabet which by this later date had become standard. These tablets were the records of a religious brotherhood and gave detailed directions for the lustration (i.e. purification) of the city. The priests were to parade around the boundaries of the city making sacrifices at the gates. Strangers were to be ordered to depart; otherwise, the instructions add on a somewhat sinister note, 'they are to be carried to where they should be carried'. After this, lustrations were to take place at various points – the fountains, the blackberry bush, etc. Then the omens were to be taken; after appropriate prayers had been said silence was to be observed so that the proper birds might appear, 'if they were gracious'. These were listed as a woodpecker, a crow or a pair of jays and they had to appear within augural lines in the sky over the city.

Today there is still a festival in Gubbio each May, The Race of the Ceri, where curious wooden poles some sixteen feet high and surmounted by statues of three saints are rushed around a gruelling uphill course by townsfolk in ancient costumes.

Another festival is still held at Monterubbiano, near Fermo and is known as 'the woodpecker chase'. This takes place on or around Whitsunday and three days of celebration include a horse race and a procession to the church for Mass, those taking part wearing ancient Roman dress. In this procession a 'woodpecker', in fact represented by a jay or magpie, is carried in a cage, tied to a branch of a cherry tree. Once again this event would seem to be a relic of an ancient rite but while the woodpecker was orginally regarded as a fertility symbol the meaning has become confused and the caged bird is now considered as a threat to the ripening fruits.

In this area of Italy the Piceni tribe are remembered today in the names of several towns which include Piceno or Picena in their titles and the province of Ascoli Piceno takes its name from that town.

The Cult of the Green Bird

Rome: The Bird of Mars

WHILE IT IS CLEAR that the cult of the woodpecker was long established in a large part of Italy before the founding of Rome, it is only after that city had become culturally mature that we can look for written records of such beliefs.

The woodpecker, we are told by Plutarch, was especially honoured and revered by the Romans and was specifically protected by them. In seeking the reasons for this it is necessary to disentangle a web of myth, ancient legends and primitive religion in which Picus appears in a variety of roles.

The people of this small city state, soon to rule most of the then known world, were practical, logically minded and not given to abstract philosophy. Their relationship with their gods tended to be down to earth, an almost contractual one in which benefits were expected in return for worship and sacrifice. At first they had no pantheon of gods, as was found in Greece, and the gods which they did recognize were not endowed with pseudo-human relationships or emotions of love, *The Cult of the Green Bird* jealousy and ambition as were the Greek gods whose adventures were handed down in traditional stories.

The history and mythology of Rome has come down to us through the literature of the Classics. This means that while our sources are diversified and the writers of that time have left us detailed accounts of the legendary founding of the city of Rome, together with the early years of the kings who came after, such sources must be looked at with some care since the Romans were always happy to borrow from the traditions of others and particularly from those of Greece. There was also a tendency to rewrite history in order to conform to the views and ambitions of the current rulers, a practice which in many parts of the world has continued down to our own time!

The leading patrician families liked to have their ancestry traced back to Rome's earliest origins, linked to Romulus and the first kings, and an aspiring author in the time of the first Caesars would be fully conscious of the desirability of emphasizing or embroidering such supposed links. In the reign of Augustus, Ovid flourished as a fashionable poet until banished and the same emperor encouraged Virgil to write the *Aeneid*, a narrative poem in the Greek style but having the birth of Rome as its theme. It was this epic poem which was universally admired throughout the Roman world and it brought together two strands of the tale of the founding of the city. The woodpecker appears in both of these, although in different guises.

The original Roman traditions told of the twins, Romulus and Remus, founding the city in 753 BC. However Greek historians as far back as the fifth

The Cult of the Green Bird

Rome: The Bird of Mars – 29

century BC were linking this event with the voyage of Aeneas from the sacked city of Troy and his arrival, after many adventures, at the land in which fate had decreed the city should be founded and which his descendants were to rule. This left an awkward gap, since Troy was known to have fallen in 1184 BC; Aeneas was therefore said to have founded a dynasty of kings at Alba Longa who filled the missing four centuries until their line culminated in the arrival of Romulus and Remus.

According to the revised version, which was given its ultimate approval by inclusion in the *Aeneid*, Aeneas landed in Latium and married the daughter of King Latinus. Virgil describes how the travellers found the aged king in this stately house, held up on a hundred columns and set amidst sacred groves. This had once been the palace of King Picus. His statue, carved in cedar, adorned the entrance hall alongside those of the other kings of old, Italus, Saturn and many more. Picus, the poet tells us, was holding the divining rod known as the lituus, wearing the trabea, the augur's purple and scarlet robe and on his left arm was the ancile, the sacred shield. he was 'Picus equum domitor', the tamer of horses.

We meet Picus again, this time in the form of a bird, as the story of Romulus and Remus and the founding of Rome unfolds. The Kingdom founded by Aeneas at Alba Longa, south of the future Rome, was ruled by a succession of twelve kings, the last being Numitor who was deposed by his brother Amulius, who took the

The Cult of the Green Bird

precaution of making Numitor's daughter, Rhea Silvia one of the Vestal Virgins so that she would remain childless. However in this plan he underestimated the god Mars, who seduced her. Ovid recounts that Silvia then had a dream. In it she saw two palm trees spring up and one, taller than the other, spread its boughs over the whole earth and up to the stars; then her uncle, the usurper, attempted to cut down the trees but they were defended by a woodpecker and a she-wolf and were saved.

The trees clearly represented Silvia's sons and in due course Romulus and Remus were born to her. Their wicked uncle ordered that they should be drowned but in a familiar outcome to such a judgement, echoing the bible story of Moses, they were washed up, unharmed, on the bank of the River Tiber and were then cared for by a wolf and a woodpecker until a shepherd found them and brought them up. On a denarius of Sextus Pompeius the twins are shown suckled by the wolf with two woodpeckers above in the sacred fig tree.

The myth portraying the ancient god-kings of Rome, in a line leading back to Saturn, was a nostalgic look back to a golden age when, as Ovid tells us, in the reign of Saturn, gold and silver, copper and iron were all kept deep in the earth's bosom and there was no need to toil behind the plough. Every good thing was plentiful, fruits abounded and wild honey was to be found in the hollow oaks.

Many religions look back to a past golden age, a paradise where man lived in harmony with the earth and nature and did not have to labour for his daily bread. In all these stories he is cast out from this state of bliss but often the place of paradise is said to continue in a distant land. In the Greek myth Cronos is deposed by his son Zeus but continues to reign in the West, in the Isles of the Blest, where Homer describes how in the plain of Elysium at the world's end, life is made its easiest for mankind. The Celts in a similar myth had their Avalon, later identified as Glastonbury but originally said to be a warm land, set in the Western Sea.

Saturn appears to have originated as an agricultural god in early Rome and was later reduced to a more humble position by Jupiter in the same manner as the downfall of Cronos was brought about by Zeus in the Greek pantheon. Picus was said to be the son of Saturn and Faunus was the son of Picus. Thus while in the Greek tradition, as we have seen, Picus handed over the sceptre to Zeus, in the Roman mythology it is Saturn, the father of Picus, who has to give way to Jupiter. In both traditions the agricultural god is deposed by the more clearly anthropomorphic god of the state religion. The simpler god of the woods and fields is downgraded but not totally deposed. This is illustrated in the story of King Numa and Picus.

Numa is recorded as the second king of Rome, who succeeded Romulus and as a priest-king laid down the foundations of the state's religion, priesthoods and public festivals. He is alleged to have been of Sabine origin but while he may well have been an historical figure it is doubtful whether he actually instituted so many of the sacred laws; some almost certainly predated his supposed reign, circa 700 BC, and others came later, brought in by the Etruscans. In any case he typifies the change in religious attitudes which were no longer simply the concern of the farmer and his family, placating the local household and agricultural gods but had become a matter for state control. Thus in the story we no longer hear of Picus as a king, enthroned in his marble palace. Instead Numa seeks him out on the Aventine Hill, at a time when it was still uninhabited and not part of the city.

Picus and Faunus, his son, were often to be found taking their ease in a grove of holm oaks on this hill, a spot so dark, as Ovid describes it, that you would say that a spirit dwelt there. In a clearing a constant stream of fresh water trickled from a spring, surrounded with green moss. The whole scene seems to conjure up the sort of sacred spot which the early Italian tribes felt to be particularly the haunt of numens who preceded the full pantheon of anthropomorphic gods who were later worshipped in formal temples.

Plutarch too records the story and describes Picus and Faunus as demi-gods; they could be likened in some ways, he tells us, to Satyrs or Pans but they could use powerful drugs and incantations and went about Italy in the same way as the Idaean Dactyls in Greece.

King Numa was anxious to find some way of controlling the thunder and torrential rain which had been assailing his people and it was for this reason that he wished to seek out the wily pair. Entering the grove he

The Cult of the Green Bird

Rome: The Bird of Mars – 33

put out bowls of wine. In due course the demi-gods drank and fell asleep and Numa had them bound. They attempted to release themselves by assuming hideous and fantastic shapes, in a manner to be expected of them in their characters as bogie men but all to no avail. The King apologises for their rough treatment and explains his problem. Faunus shakes his horns and says they are only rustic deities whose rule is in the mountains; nevertheless they could help. Picus agrees with him but very sensibly insists that their shackles should be taken off before matters proceed.

At this point two versions of the story are offered. According to Plutarch the rustic pair then foretell the future and teach Numa the charm against thunder which was still practised in Plutarch's own time (i.e. in the first century AD). However in an alternative version followed by Ovid and also mentioned by Plutarch as a possible variation, Picus and Faunus say that Jupiter is in charge of thunder but by means of spells which are too secret to be revealed they can induce the god to appear. This is done and the now petrified king makes his request. After some tough negotiations, made necessary by Jupiter's initial demand for human sacrifice, the charm against thunder made up of hair, onions and pilchards is revealed. The god withdraws in a jovial mood and the next day at sun rise lets loose three claps of thunder as a token of good faith and sends down to earth a shield (the ancile). Numa had eleven copies made of these shields so that the original might be less at risk from theft or any chance destruction.

The Cult of the Green Bird

The twelve Ancilia were given for safe keeping to a college of priests known as the Salii. In some traditions it was said to be Mars who sent down the anciles. The Salii were named from the latin word 'salire' to leap, on account of the vigorous leaping and jumping which took place in their sacred dances. They would seem to have born a close similarity to the Cretan Curetes; both groups were made up of young men who danced energetically, clashing their shields with swords or drumsticks. The Salii performed their rites in March, the month of Mars, dancing the sacred three step through the streets and driving out the old year and bringing in the new. They chanted the Salian hymns, invoking different gods to bestow a fruitful harvest, seeking to encourage the crops to grow tall with their lusty leaping. At the same time the New Year was the start of the fighting season and the blessing of Mars was sought for the Roman army. Later this martial aspect of the god became predominant. The Roman infantry assembled on the Campus Martius outside the City, an echo of the fields in Umbria said to belong to the Woodpecker of Mars.

The inclusion of Picus in the tale of King Numa's acquisition of the ancile suggests a link with the Sabine culture which mingled with that of the Latin peoples in the City when the Sabines infiltrated Rome as they undoubtedly did even if the story of the rape of the Sabine women is discounted. Numa Pompilius was probably a Sabine and a true historical figure, even if he was not responsible for all the institutions attributed

The Cult of the Green Bird

I once a king and chief · now am the tree-barks thief :

ever twixt trunk and leaf · chasing the prey ·

The Cult of the Green Bird

36 – Rome: The Bird of Mars

Opposite: 2. *The Woodpecker Tapestry by William Morris.*

The Tapestry was woven at Morris & Company's workshops, Merton Abbey, Surrey, in 1885.

*It illustrates Picus as a green woodpecker in the branches of a fruit tree and is based on Ovid's story of the ancient Italian king who, having spurned the advances of the enchantress Circe, was turned by her into a bird. (*Metamorphoses *book XIV)*

The text above and below the central panel refers to this story but it seems to typify the wider theme in which the role of the green woodpecker in mythology is constantly moving between that of a god, a king or simply an oracular bird.

© The William Morris Gallery,
Walthamstow, London

to him. His association with Picus can be seen to stem from the traditions of his people who emanated from the area around Picenum.

Ovid tells us that Picus, presumably while still a king or demi-god, fell into the clutches of Circe. She was a goddess who was also a sorceress and had poisoned her husband, the king of the Sarmatians and was depicted as a lady of undoubted charms. Picus seems to have been wise to resist her advances even though it was her habit to turn those who rejected her into animals. Circe duly turned him into a bird but this seems a minor inconvenience which was no doubt worthwhile as a means of escape from such a virago. In other stories he is said to have married Pomona, goddess of fruits, a much more suitable bride for an agricultural god.

A ceremony observed at the birth of a Roman child involved the preparation of a couch for Pilumnus and Picumnus; they brought the fire of life to the newborn infant and were expected to stay in the house until it was known that the child was likely to live. Pilumnus, said to be the brother of Picus, seems in effect to have been his double and was perhaps introduced to maintain the tradition of twins as with Romulus and Remus. Pilumnus took his name from 'pilum', a javelin, perhaps representing a thunderbolt, or the derivation may have been merely phallic.

The Cult of the Green Bird   As the Roman Empire expanded, the legions and the officials of the civil administration took the state religion with them, represented primarily by Jupiter Optimus Maximus and later often coupled with worship of the Emperor; Mars and Mercury were also popular. Loyalty to the state religion was expected and numerous altars and inscriptions have survived to show that in the towns and garrisons due note was taken of this requirement. Nevertheless other religions were always tolerated and local gods allowed to blend with those of Rome.

A notable exception to this tolerance was Druidism which amongst the Celts was considered to be nationalistic and a subversive influence against Roman rule. In Gaul it was ruthlessly suppressed and the same policy adopted in Britain when this country was invaded. Tacitus has left us a vivid description of the governor Paulinus advancing towards the island of Anglesey, the Druid stronghold in AD 61. In a well-known passage Tacitus describes how on reaching the Menai Straits the Romans were astonished and at first terrified by the sight of their adversaries on the opposite shore. The armed Celts were drawn up in ranks through which ran groups of women carrying lighted torches, their long hair flying in the wind; behind them the Druids stood by their sacrificial fires, their hands raised in prayer for help against their foes. Recovering themselves the Romans crossed the Straits and fell upon the Britons casting them into their own fires and then advanced through the island until news of a more serious rising by Boudicca in the south forced Paulinus to turn back.

It is unfortunate that the authors of this time have left us very little information regarding the actual beliefs and practices of the Druids. We know that they regarded

The Cult of the Green Bird

3. The Thetford Ring.

A gold ring from the Thetford Treasure, the bezel holding a glass gem, flanked by two birds resembling woodpeckers.

© The British Museum

the oak as sacred and John Aubrey states that 'the woodpecker was much esteemed by the Druids for divination'. It is not clear what his authority was for this remark but considering the ancient links of this bird with the oak it seems likely to be accurate. The Druids apart, the rural population of Gaul and Britain clearly had many agricultural and nature gods which blended comfortably with those which the Romans brought with them.

An archeological find in England has produced evidence that the woodpecker was associated with a religious cult during the Roman occupation. In November 1979 a hoard of Roman silver and jewellery was unearthed near Thetford in Norfolk. These items, which came to be known as the Thetford Treasure, eventually reached the British Museum and consisted of silver plate and gold jewellery, the latter including a ring with a bezel modelled in the form of a small vase supported by birds, convincingly identified by Dr Johns as woodpeckers.* The ring did not show any sign of wear and it is not known whether it was made locally or abroad. The treasure would seem to have been buried towards the end of the fourth or beginning of the fifth century AD. The political scene was often turbulent as Rome's grip on Britain weakened or religious persecution could have prompted concealment of the hoard.

By the time the treasure came to be assessed the site

---

* C. Johns & T. Potter, *The Thetford Treasure*, London 1983.

where it was discovered had been built upon, so it was not possible to carry out any archeological investigation to ascertain whether the site showed any indications of having been a temple or centre of a cult. Many of the silver pieces were inscribed with references to Faunus, together with Celtic names for this god or similar local deities.

It cannot be determined whether the gold items, including the woodpecker ring, were associated with the same cult as the silver items or were merely buried alongside them for concealment in time of trouble, nor will it ever be known whether they were in transit or buried close to the place of their use. All that can be deduced with any certainty is that the woodpecker still had a place in Romano-British society of that time as a symbol associated with Mars or his attendant minor gods, Faunus, Picus or Pan and it seems likely that the ring was made for use in some ritual of worship or prophecy.

The Messengers of the Gods

Divination

AWARENESS of a god or gods must always have brought with it a desire by man to know his own destiny and if possible to influence it. The gods could be approached by prayer and their goodwill sought by offerings and sacrifices but the urge to look into the future and learn their will by some immediate and direct means must have given rise to the practice of divination early in man's development; this desire would be accentuated as a more evolved lifestyle gave him more choice over his own actions. For the early hunters, decisions were limited; they invoked the aid of the gods of the land and of the chase and sought to propitiate the spirits of the animals they hunted. Later generations however, had many more decisions to make. A farmer needed to know the best time to sow and reap the harvest. As permanent settlements were formed the most suitable sites had to be selected for towns and villages; tribes had to choose between peace and war, and as civilization took shape individuals had freedom of choice within their own lives as to marriage, the making of journeys and the acquisition of wealth.

The Cult of the Green Bird

It was natural for earth-bound man to look upwards to seek signs from the gods, to the night sky which gave birth to divination by astrology and by day to the flight and behaviour of birds; they were nearer to the heavens than man and gifted with a freedom of movement which he did not possess.

Plutarch expressed this in one of his plays:

> Birds by their quickness and intelligence and their alertness in acting upon every thought, are a ready instrument for the use of God, who can prompt their movements, their cries and songs, their pauses or wind-like flights, thus bidding some men check and others pursue to the end their course of action or ambitions. It is on this account that Euripides calls birds in general 'heralds of the gods' while Socrates speaks of making himself 'a fellow servant with swans'.

Divination through birds seems to have been very widespread. In the Greek language the word for an omen comes from the same root as that for a bird and it appears to have been the principal method used in Arabia, in the countries which now form modern Turkey and in many parts of Italy. We have limited direct evidence as to which birds were used for this purpose, but bearing in mind the woodpecker's close association with Zeus in the Near East and its position as the bird of Mars in Italy, it seems certain that its appearance was widely sought when the auspices were taken and it was considered significant if the bird appeared spontaneously.

The Cult of the Green Bird

Both Horace and Plutarch refer to omens divined

from the direction of the woodpecker's flight and in well-wooded country it must have been sufficiently familiar for this purpose without being too commonplace. However with the growth of cities and substantial towns, such sightings must have become more difficult and this perhaps accounts for the growth of the practice of keeping chickens and observing their behaviour when released to feed. A total failure to feed was considered to be a very grave portent indeed, although this failed to intimidate one Roman general before a battle, who in response to the augur's report of this omen said 'let them drink instead' and had them drowned. It would seem that it was Etruscan influences which modified but did not orginate these methods.

The Romans in all matters of art and religion borrowed ideas freely from other nations in preference to creating their own distinctive culture and theories. The qualities which turned a small tribe into the rulers of an empire were applied to religion as to any other matter which concerned the government and the state; to the Roman mind, order and reason were paramount virtues and the arts of divination were codified by decree and fixed by long tradition. Strict rules ordained the place where the auspices might be taken, the participants and the method of taking them. Only the actual interpretation maintained an aura of mystery, as this was reserved for the members of the College of Augurs, an august body, said to have been founded by Romulus himself.

King Picus wore the trappings of an augur. It was he who is said to have first carried the lituus, the staff of

The Cult of the Green Bird

office carried by members of the College and used by Romulus to mark out the templum (the space marked out for taking the auspices). In actual fact it is possible that this was of Etrurian origin and was imported into Roman culture at a later date. Cicero describes it as a crooked wand, slightly curved at the top and called a lituus because of its resemblance to a trumpet. He records that the original lituus was placed in the temple of the Salii on the Palatine Hill and was the only object to be saved when the temple was sacked by the Gauls in 390 BC. The lituus survives today as the crozier carried by a bishop of the Roman or Anglican churches.

Under the early kings of Rome there were three augurs, all selected from patrician families. In 300 BC as the plebeian classes began to gain some say in matters of state, the college was enlarged to nine members and it was decreed that five of these should be plebs. Finally in the first century BC the number rose to fifteen but by this time the office was largely an honorary one. Cicero was himself elected to the college in 53 BC and wrote a treatise on divination in which he discusses the origins and justification of the practice. In the opening passage he is unable to resist pointing out the superiority of the logical Roman mind:

> There is an ancient belief, handed down to us even from mythical times and firmly established by the general agreement of the Roman people and of all nations that divination of some kind exists among men; this the Greeks call foresight and knowledge of future events. A really splendid and helpful thing it is – if only such a

faculty exists – since by its means men may approach very near to the power of the gods. And, just as we Romans have done many other things better than the Greeks, so we have excelled them in giving to this most extraordinary gift a name, which we have derived from 'divi', a word meaning 'gods', whereas, according to Plato's interpretation, they have derived it from 'furor', a word meaning 'frenzy'.

This passage seems to typify the difference in approach of the two nations. To the Greeks the will of the gods was to be revealed by a heightening of consciousness induced by various means, including hallucinating drugs and fasting. In the ordered Roman world divination was something to be practiced in public by sober officials of the state working to well-established rules. Cicero in his treatise, having discussed the pros and cons of divination and in spite of being himself an augur, finally comes down on the side of those disbelieving in divination but seems to approve its continuation as a matter of political expediency.

Only the king, or later the senior magistrate present at a gathering, was allowed to seek a sign and he was said to 'have the auspices'. Originally at least the signs sought were always connected with the behaviour of birds as is made clear from the word 'auspices' which is derived from 'avi-spicium', meaning literally 'bird watching'.

The magistrate would take his seat in the open; in Rome a special site, the Auguraculum, was set aside for this purpose on the Capitol. He was accompanied by an augur who would indicate the quarter of the sky in which the sign was to be sought, the templum, marking it out with the lituus in a ceremony originated by Romulus. He would then sit blindfolded while the magistrate scanned the ordained portion of the heavens. Certain birds were to be studied for their calls; pitch, intonation and frequency being significant: these were known as 'oscines' and included the raven, crow and owl. Other birds such as the eagle and vulture were watched for their manner of flying ('alites') and here speed, direction and height were noted. It is not recorded into which category the woodpecker was considered to fall; there are several references to the bird's direction of flight having a significance but it is difficult to imagine that its distinctive call would have been ignored, so perhaps it was accepted in either category.

Once a bird or birds of one of the approved categories appeared in the templum, the magistrate would note their behaviour and it was then for the augur alone to interpret the meaning of the sign. Clearly this gave him considerable power and at times of national crisis his decree could be crucial. The auspices were taken in public but the rules governing the interpretation were secret so that the office of augur must always have been politically important and the need for men of the right shade of political opinion must have been as vital to Rome's rulers as the appointment of sympathetically minded bishops was to medieval monarchs.

The Cult of the Green Bird

The formal consultation of the augurs was undertaken before any act of state and signs thus given in answer to a specific request were known as 'impetrativa'. However, it was also recognised that the gods could offer signs spontaneously ('ostenta') and Pliny in his *Natural History* recorded an instance which shows that the unusual behaviour of one of the recognized birds of omen was taken very seriously and that the woodpecker was one of these. According to Pliny, the City Praetor, Aelius Tubero, was giving judgement from the bench in the forum when a woodpecker landed on his head – an unusual occurrence in itself, but it remained there so fearlessly that the praetor was able to raise his hand and catch the bird. Such an event clearly called for interpretation by the augurs and when consulted they declared that disaster was portended to the empire if the bird were to be released but to the praetor if it were killed. Tubero at once tore the bird in pieces and, Pliny informs us, not long afterwards he fulfilled the portent, although we are not told the precise fate of the unfortunate praetor. Faced with this dilemma and imbued with the sense of duty to the state which was no doubt expected of any high-born Roman, he must have felt that no other option was open to him. Perhaps his own subsequent fate was one reserved for those laying violent hands on the gods' winged messenger.

The Greek philosophers whose influence spread to Rome, on the whole approved of divination and the Stoics in particular by their conception of 'providence', gave it their blessing. They considered that everything in the universe was permeated by an all-embracing power and for that reason there could be a sympathetic reaction between different parts of it and different forms

The Cult of the Green Bird

of creation; thus the divine will could be illustrated by such manifestations as the flight and behaviour of birds.

The opponents of divination argued that if all events were previously ordained, divination could have no function since it gave the individual the opportunity to change those very events which had been foretold. This of course raises an age-old and fundamental argument concerning any attempt to look into the future and is countered by the hypothesis that both divination and the subsequent actions of one responding to it form links in the chain of causation and both are foreordained.

Belief in divination has been given a new validity in the twentieth century by the work of Carl Jung and his concept of synchronicity, which he defined as meaningful coincidences. These, according to Jung are achieved through the archetypes, the first principles governing the forces and forms of all creation. In his work on the subject* he discusses a case in which the wife of one of his patients was forewarned of the quite unexpected death of her husband by the appearance of a flock of birds at her window, this being something which had previously occurred on the deaths of her mother and grandmother. According to Jung's theory, divination functions by man's unconscious linking through the archetypes with apparently random patterns in nature. In the case which he cites however, as in augury, it would seem necessary to go a stage further to explain

---

* C. G. Jung, *Synchronicity*, Routledge & Kegan Paul, trans. 1972

the arrival of the flock of birds at the wife's window, an event which for the third occasion was presumably too unusual to be simply a random pattern of nature. It would appear that the collective unconscious of the birds needed to be influenced to bring about the meaningful coincidence and this seems the logical combination linking Jung's theory of 'archetypes' and the 'sympatheia' of the Stoics.

Thus in the present century modern theories have taken us back to beliefs in divination which were current in classical times. Before this we have to peer into the mists of mythology and ancient customs handed down by oral tradition. In the intervening centuries between the fall of Rome and modern times such traditions were largely relegated to folklore.

The Cult of the Green Bird

Oracles

ORACLES, although used for the same basic purpose as divination, that is to say to ascertain the will of the gods or to glimpse the future, must have developed later than divination and lacked the latter's general accessibility. Divination could be practised anywhere but consulting an oracle involved visiting a particular sacred spot or an individual priest or shaman. This can be compared to visiting a Christian holy shrine as against prayer in general.

Even when divination was formalized and in the case of augury by the state was carried out in a place set aside for it, a question was posed to the gods but it was not known what form the answer would take. The awaited sign came from without and its manifestation was uncertain. Consultation with an oracle on the other hand made use of a known medium: only the answer was in doubt.

There is firm evidence of an oracle associated with the woodpecker in the writings of Dionysios of Halicarnassus, a Greek by birth, who wrote a history of Rome in the first century BC. Describing how most of the cities of the ancient Italian tribes had disappeared he wrote that Tiora, called Matiene, was situated in the Apennines: 'Here there is said to have been an oracle of Mars of great antiquity. It is reported to have been similar in character to the fabled oracle at Dodona, except that whereas at Dodona it was said that a dove on a sacred oak gave oracles, among the Aborigines the oracles were given in like fashion by a god-sent bird

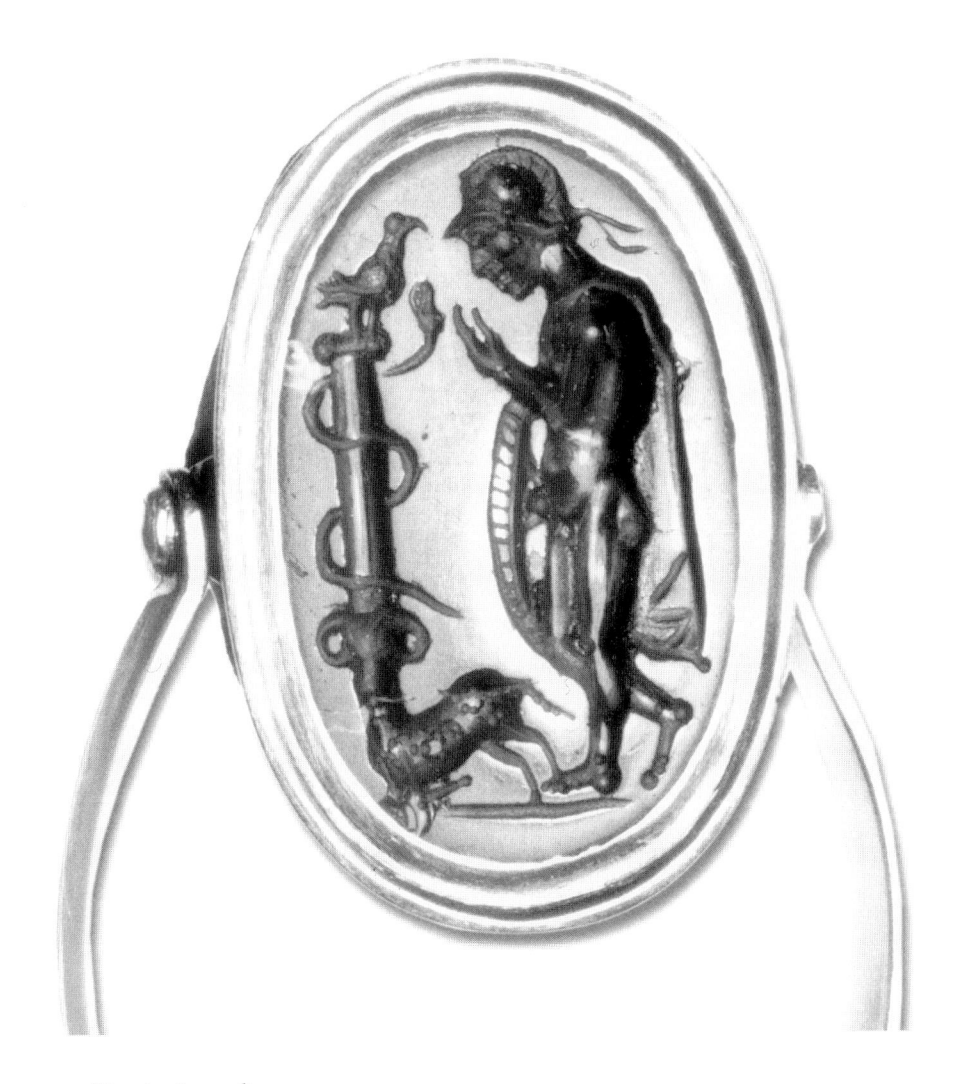

4. Single Intaglio.

A Carnelian ringstone, in intaglio; Roman Republican, second or first century BC.

Fitzwilliam Museum Collection.

© *The Institute of Archaeology, Oxford.*

The Cult of the Green Bird

The Messengers of the Gods – 53

called by them Picus (the Greeks name it Dryokolaptes) which appears on a wooden pillar'.

This description is matched by images shown on a number of gemstones dating from the first or second century BC which are preserved in various museums. One, now in the Hanover Museum, shows a warrior, holding a shield, in front of a pillar, on top of which is the bird which the man appears to be consulting; his hand is uplifted towards the bird and a snake is wound round the post, at the bottom of which is a ram. Another ringstone in the Fitzwilliam Museum at Cambridge shows an almost identical scene; a young warrior leans forward towards the bird on the post, his hand raised, and he seems to be either addressing the bird or listening to it. The snake and the ram are again shown. There are other examples which follow much the same pattern and the fact that so many have survived leads one to the conclusion that either the Tiora oracle was widely famed or else that it was not unique.

No knowledge has come down to us as to how the oracle was consulted. It has been suggested that the doves at the Greek oracle at Dodona, which Dionysios compares to Tiora Matiene, were actually carrier pigeons who brought the temple priests advance information of events which the priests were then able to present as foreknowledge. This would then be confirmed when the news reached the area by normal channels but this explanation could not apply to a woodpecker. Was the bird tethered to the sacred pillar or trained to alight on it? Were the questions answered by the cries or gestures of the bird or did a priest interpret them? We cannot be certain.

The Cult of the Green Bird

The addition of the ram and the snake to all these gems must also be considered. Dr Harrison took the ram to be a sacrificial one but the animal is not tethered and there is no sign of an altar or implement of sacrifice and it seems as likely that it is represented in these scenes because of the association of the rural gods Picus and Faunus with flocks and fertility. Also it must be remembered that astrology had become fashionable in the period to which these rings are attributed and the ram is the sign of Aries of which Mars is the ruling planet.

As to the snake, that creature's symbolism is so wide and varied that we can only conjecture what its meaning is here. Winding around the post it may indicate that the woodpecker's post stems, like a tree, from the earth. Alternatively it may be a symbol of fertility or, on a different level, may represent the wisdom to be sought from the oracle.

We can be certain of none of these things but what is clear is that an oracle, or oracles, of the Tiora Matiene type must have had a considerable following for many years.

5. Another example of a ringstone showing a warrior consulting an oracular bird, probably Italian first century BC.

© The British Museum

The Cult of the Green Bird

The Messengers of the Gods – 55

The Rain-Bird

THE GREEN WOODPECKER'S REPUTATION as a rain-bird is extremely widespread in the folklore of Europe. In England no bird has more regional and colloquial names and many of these refer to the idea that the bird's call forecasts rain. Thus we have:

Rain-bird
Rainfowl
Rain-pie (Shropshire)
Wet Bird (Somerset)
Weather-hatcher (Sussex)

On the Continent we find:

Pic de la Pluie (Rain-woodpecker) France
Avocat de Meunier (Miller's Counsellor) France
Rågnfågal (Rain-bird) Sweden
Giessvogel (Pouring-rain-bird) Germany

In France the familiar 'laugh' is rendered as 'Pluie-pluie-pluie', thus making the bird literally call for rain and a proverb from the Eure and Loire districts says:

Lorsque le pivert crie
Il annonce la pluie

(i.e. When the woodpecker cries he is foretelling rain.)

In Italy there are several sayings on a similar theme:

> Co' Ipigozzo per aria'l cria
> La borasca ne vien via (from Venetia)

and

> Quand el picozz picozza
> O che l'e vent, o che l'e gozza (from Milan)

and another more general prediction of hard weather from Venetia:

> Quando canta il pigozzo di Gennaio
> Tieni a mano il pagliaio

(i.e. When the woodpecker sings in January, keep your fodder until the morrow.)

A French tale from the Gironde gives the following tradition as an explanation for the green woodpecker constantly calling out for rain:

> There is a legend that the peasants never fail to relate each time the green woodpecker, while flying from one tree to another, gives its hearty laugh 'plui-plui'. They say that when the good God decided to dig out the sea, the rivers and the springs, He gave this work to the birds of the air. They all set to work except the green woodpecker which did not stir from his place. Therefore, when the task was completed, the good God declared that the woodpecker, because it had refused to dig out the earth with its beak, should dig into wood for all

time; and because it took no part in the digging out of the earth's reservoirs, it would never drink any water except the rain as it drops from the air. For this reason the unfortunate bird never ceases to invoke the rain clouds with its significant cry of 'plui-plui', and always maintains an upright posture, so that its open beak can catch the drops which fall from the clouds.

This is not the only story in which the woodpecker incurs God's displeasure and the significance of this is discussed elsewhere. The immediate question is why the bird has become so closely associated with rain and is said to be either calling for it or more often actually forecasting its impending arrival. At the level of natural history there appears to be no evidence that the green woodpecker calls more often or with greater vigour when rain is approaching; indeed he seems to like nothing better on a fine sunny day in spring than to sit high up in a tree facing the sun with apparent enjoyment and giving forth a cheerful 'yaffle' from time to time.

Some birds may truly be used to forecast rain, as for example the swallow, which flies high in fair weather following the insects on which it feeds, while in moist air it will skim low over ground in pursuit of its prey. The weather does not change the feeding pattern of the woodpecker in this way, but ants are its favourite food and these are said always to make their nests over underground water and to sink shafts, sometimes to a considerable depth, to obtain water. It is conceivable that early man used this knowledge to sink his own wells and observing the woodpecker's fondness for these spots assumed he was seeking water. In this context there is a reference in French folklore to the bird digging up ant-hills to procure water for his clients, the millers.

One of the French names for the woodpecker, as has already been noted is the Miller's Counsellor. At first sight this must relate to the need to supply power to a water-driven mill, but lack of rain will also bring about a dearth of corn and thus of grain and finally of bread. There are many folk tales which involve the withholding of bread and the consequent punishment of the withholder. In one version, when Jesus and St. Peter were wandering upon earth, they came to the house of an old woman, called Gertrude, who was baking with her head covered by a red linen cap. Christ begged for a small loaf and the old woman agreed to give them one and took a very small piece of dough and rolled it out but it grew and filled the girdle. Thinking this too generous she took a smaller piece and rolled it out but again it filled the girdle; then she took a third piece, even smaller, but still it grew to the same size. At this the old woman's patience was exhausted and she declared that as all the bannocks were too big her visitors should have nothing. Angered by the woman's meanness, Jesus told her that as a punishment she should become a bird, seeking her food between bark and bole and have nothing to drink except when it rained. Immediately the old woman was turned into a woodpecker and flew up the chimney, where the soot turned all her feathers black, except for her red cap, and ever since she has been forced to search for her food by delving into the bark of trees and she calls for rain to quench her constant thirst.

The Cult of the Green Bird

This story obviously relates to the black woodpecker which is known as Gertrude's Fowl in Scandinavia. According to Grimm, Gertrude is the Christian substitute for Freya and while Thor was of course the god of thunder, he was never recorded as sending rain when this was asked for but only storms when he was angry; Freya, however, was a weeping goddess who wandered the world seeking her husband who had forsaken her and shedding tears, and thus she was identified as a provider of rain.

Variations of the tale of Gertrude are common and in an English version it is the greedy daughter of a baker who wishes to keep all the bread for herself and is punished by being turned into an owl, a tradition touched on by Shakespeare in Hamlet. However, in a version from Wales, Christ asked a woman for food and water; she refused to give him either and was thereupon turned into a bird and told by Christ that in future she would only eat of the stuff to be found between the wood and the bark of trees and would drink only when it rained. The bird was not named but as the great black woodpecker is not known in Wales, it would seem clear that the green 'rain-bird' was intended. This story, according to Trevelyan, was told not only in North Wales but also in Carmarthenshire and Pembrokeshire during the nineteenth century. James Montgomery (1771–1854) is said to be referring to this legend in his poem to the woodpecker:

Rap, rap, rap, rap, I hear thy knocking bill,
Then thy strange outcry, when the woods are still.

Thus am I ever labouring for my bread,
And thus give thanks to find my table spread.

This need, not simply for rain, but for gentle showers to ripen the crops, is beautifully illustrated by the prayer of an old Estonian farmer which was taken down verbatim by John Gutslaff and published in 1644; in the English translation of Grimm's Teutonic Mythology it is given as follows:

> Dear Thunder (Woda Picker), we offer to thee an ox that hath two horns and four cloven hoofs, and we would pray thee for our ploughing and sowing, that our straw be copper-red, our grain be golden-yellow. Push elsewhither all the thick black clouds, over great fens, high forests and wildernesses. But unto us ploughers and sowers give a fruitful season and sweet rain.
> Holy thunder (Poka Picken) guard our seed-field that it bear good straw below, good ears above and good rain within.

Neither Grimm nor Frazer, in *The Golden Bough*, both of whom noted this passage, associated 'Picker' and 'Picken' with the woodpecker: Grimm portrays Picker as a local god of thunder and agriculture and relates him back to Zeus. However, Rendel Harris makes out a strong case for identifying 'Picker' with the woodpecker, showing the similarity to the Scandinavian names for the bird 'traepikka' or 'traepikker' and the Saxon 'pikka', also some of the French names derived from the Latin Picus.

The quotation is discussed by Armstrong in his *Folklore of Birds* and he points out that according to some authorities, Pikker was never a personal god in the mythology of Estonia, although he figures in fairy tales as the son of thunder. It would seem that Pikker the god may well have been a romantic creation from the time of the Renaissance but at the level of folklore at least the connection between the woodpecker, thunder and rain is well established and although Harris's conclusions, linking the woodpecker with characters from mythology and folklore are often tenuous, on this occasion his ideas seem sound.

In general the actual habits of the woodpecker seem to offer no explanation for its universal reputation as a rain-bird and although its call can convincingly be rendered as 'pluie-pluie-pluie' in French, there is no similar link between this call and the word for 'rain' in other European languages. To find an explanation it is necessary to return to the beginnings of the green bird's cult and look again, both at its links with the invention of the plough and at its association with Zeus, traditionally the god of thunder and of rain.

We have seen the green woodpecker's connections with man's first attempt to grow crops and to till the soil. This called for the availability of wild strains of corn to provide seed, implements to break up the ground and settled habitations but it also meant that for the first time man became dependent on a suitable climate and rainfall for his crops to grow. Before this, lakes or rivers could supply his needs for water and providing these did not dry up, it was not important to him when the rains came or whether they came in violent storms or gentle showers. With the birth of agriculture all this changed: rain was essential to germinate the seed but a severe storm later in the year could ruin the harvest. For the first time it became essential, rather than just desirable, to anticipate the moods of the weather and man looked to his gods to bless each stage of his enterprise and to the messengers of these gods to prophesy the most propitious times to sow and to reap.

Mars, originally an agricultural god rather than one of war, might well have been turned to as a forecaster or provider of rain by farmers throughout Italy where he was generally revered; however, by the time of Roman domination there is very little evidence that Mars was considered to have any specific link with rain but only with the general concept of fertility of both animals and crops, although a stone, the lapis manalis, was kept near the temple of Mars outside the city and this was brought within the walls to ensure rain in times of drought. It seems more probable that in order to find the roots of the green woodpecker's reputation as a rain bird throughout the folklore of medieval Europe we must go back to Zeus and the connection of that god and the bird with the oak tree.

The beginnings of agriculture coincided with a period when climatic conditions favoured the oak and it was the dominant tree in the great forests which spread across the temperate zone throughout Europe and the Near East. The oak is a tall tree with rough bark and is more prone to being struck by lightning than smooth-barked trees such as the beech. It is thought that this is because a film of water develops on the smooth bark of trees such as the beech during heavy rain and this

The Cult of the Green Bird

will conduct the lightning to earth; the rough bark of the oak will prevent this natural lightning conductor from forming. Thus it became a tree particularly associated with thunder and this, coupled with its size and longevity made it an object of veneration among all the Aryan races. To be in a thunder storm in a forest is an awe-inspiring experience and not without its dangers. Men would have noticed that tall oaks were singled out for lightning strikes and with the accompanying clap of thunder and drenching rain, it must have seemed that these trees were indeed the abode of powerful spirits, and as religion became more anthropomorphic they became sacred to the principal gods of many races.

The links between the oak, rain, thunder and the leading male god are to be found in the mythology of very many nations. The Greek Zeus, to whom the oak was sacred, was often depicted carrying a thunderbolt and there was an image of Earth praying to him for rain on the Acropolis in Athens. In the same way Jupiter, the Roman counterpart of Zeus, was given the same attributes and we have been left a vivid description of noble Roman matrons walking bare-footed up the Capitoline Hill with streaming hair and pure minds to pray to Jupiter for rain: 'and straightway', we are told, 'it rained bucketsful, then or never and everybody returned dripping like drowned rats.' Donar, among the German races and Thor in Scandinavia were the gods of thunder and the oak tree was sacred to them, although as we have seen, it was Freya in Scandinavia who was looked to for rain.

How then has the woodpecker become the rain-bird?

Although frequently appearing in classical mythology it is not recorded in Greek or Roman literature as a provider or foreteller of rain; rather it is concerned with fertility and divination. It is in the realm of folklore that the woodpecker is known as the rain-bird throughout Europe and there are various possible explanations.

In many parts of the world thunder was said to be produced by a mythical bird which made the noise of the thunder by clapping its wings and the flash of the lightning with a wink of its eye. This belief was common among the Indians of North and South America and in many parts of Africa. Rendel Harris traced the development of the thunder bird through a stage of half bird, half god, into a fully anthropomorphic god in various parts of the world and he considered that the eagle (a bird associated with both Zeus and Jupiter) had a predecessor as a thunder bird in the woodpecker. According to Harris this could be either the black or green species, as both have red heads, red plumage being a common feature of such creatures, real or mythical.

This theory ties in with the fact that the green woodpecker was known in Babylon as the Axe of Ishtar, an axe being a common symbol for a thunderbolt, later associated with Zeus and Donar. It has also been suggested that the woodpecker actually appeared to be making thunder by drumming but it must be born in mind that it is only the green species which is known as the rain-bird and this is only an occasional drummer.

A picture emerges of a thunder bird gradually displaced by gods who control the weather. In Italy Jupiter takes over these functions, while the woodpecker becomes the bird of Mars. However, the bird retains its associations with the oak and because of its identification with fertility and ploughing a tradition lives on that it is concerned with the successful growing of crops and therefore with rain. Perhaps too, there are echoes of the original Picus, who before the reign of the Olympian gods would have been approached for a fruitful harvest.

Thus the origins of the green woodpecker's reputation as the rain-bird lie deep in the past but for the British sub-species (which shows very minor differences when compared to its continental cousins) science appears to have endorsed folklore, since early in this century our own woodpecker was officially designated *Picus viridis pluvius*!

The Cult of the Green Bird

The Legend of the Springwort

SINCE THE EARLIEST TIMES man has recognized the beneficial effects of certain plants and a substantial mythology has built up to surround many herbs with an aura of magical and healing properties. Alongside this there has arisen a tradition of plants containing such amazing powers that their identification is uncertain and the quest to find them becomes all-important; of these a plant which gives its holder the ability to open any lock or door is a persistent theme and it is usually given the name springwort although also known as wonder-flower, key-flower, moon-wort or spring-wurzel. This plant is constantly associated with the woodpecker, the green or sometimes the black species, and the aid of the bird is required to locate it.

In classical times the elder Pliny referred to woodpeckers in his *Natural History* and goes on:

> There is a common belief that when wedges are driven into their holes by a shepherd, the birds, by applying a kind of grass make them slip out again. Trebius states that if you drive a nail or wedge with as much force as

you like into a tree in which a woodpecker has a nest, when the bird perches on it it at once springs out again with a creak of the tree.

In another passage of the same work Pliny goes back three hundred years from his own time and cites Theophrastus, a Greek writing in the fourth century BC as his source for the same legend, adding: 'Although these tales are incredible, yet they fill us with wonder, and force us to admit that there is still much truth in them.'

It occurs again as the Samir legend in the Arabian Nights in which a nest, blocked this time by a stone, is opened by means of Sesame, the magic herb brought by the bird.

These beliefs must have been extraordinarily persistent and widespread as we find the same tales cropping up in mid-European folklore, and in England John Aubrey refers to it in his *Natural History of Wiltshire* written during the second half of the seventeenth century. He wrote:

> Sir Bennet Hoskins, Baronet, told me that his keeper at his parks at Morehampton in Herefordshire, did, for experiment sake, drive an iron naile thwart the hole of the woodpecker's nest, there being a tradition that the damme will bring some leafe to open it. He layed at the bottome of the tree a cleane sheet, and before many hours passed the naile came out, and he found a leafe lying by it on the sheete. Quaere the shape or figure of the leafe. They say the moon-wort will do such stranger things to be seen in the world than are between London and Stanes.

Later writers may have poured scorn on these tales but clearly we are dealing with a very strong and deeply-rooted tradition for it to have survived for well over two thousand years with the main features unaltered.

The name given to the plant varies, sometimes it is purely mythical, at others its properties are ascribed to plants known to botanists. Some times it is said to be the root that is all important, at other times it is the flower. In classical references it was said to be the peony, named after Paeon, god of healing.

John Gerard published a herbal in England in 1597 and this flower is listed in it, but Gerard does not attach any specific healing properties to it. He quotes from the classical writers describing the traditions that the seeds of the plant glow like candles in the night making it easy for shepherds to locate it, and the danger that he who first plucks the plant will (as with the mandrake) perish and for this reason a string should be attached to it and a hungry dog tied to the other end which is then enticed with a piece of meat so that it pulls up the plant and takes the danger on itself: finally that it must be gathered by night to avoid one's eyes being attacked by the woodpecker who guards the plant. Gerard is extremely scornful of all these tales which he calls most vain and frivolous.

In the next century however, Nicholas Culpeper also published a herbal and his attitude seems more ambivalent; for him astrology and the planetary influences of each herb were important and he identifies moonwort as a type of fern which the moon 'owns', as he puts it, and recommends it for healing all kinds of wounds. He adds:

Moonwort is a herb which (they say) will open locks, and unshoe such horses as tread upon it. This some laugh to scorn, and those no small fools neither; but country people that I know call it unshoe the horse. Besides, I have heard commanders say, that on White Down in Devonshire, near Tiverton, there were found thirty horseshoes, pulled off from the feet of the Earl of Essex's horses, being there drawn up in a body, many of them being but newly shod and no reason known, which caused much admiration: and the herb described usually grows upon heaths.

In this passage Nicholas Culpeper can be seen to be of two minds. Magic and witchcraft were still taken seriously by 'country people' as he calls them but scientific minds were beginning to question such things; he reports the legend but adds that many scoff at it. Nevertheless he himself had fought in the Civil War on the side of Parliament and he was clearly impressed by the tale which he appears to have heard directly from officers in the Roundhead army.

In the middle of the nineteenth century Jacob Grimm set himself the task of bringing together the scattered mythology of all the Teutonic races, embracing the Scandinavian and Saxon races from Iceland to the Danube and the result was the publication of his *Teutonic Mythology*. In it he refers to the wonderflower or keyflower and relates the usual tale of the need to find the nest of a black or green woodpecker in order to locate the herb. Once again the nest hole must be closed, with a wooden bung, whereupon the bird will seek out the wonderflower and return with it to the nest, holding it in her bill in front of the bung which forthwith flies out. The watcher must then leap out of hiding and frighten the bird with a shout so that it drops the herb or else a white or red cloth must be placed under the nest in which case she will drop it on that after using it.

Grimm quotes Conrad von Megenberg who says that in Latin the bird is called 'merops' (i.e. bee-eater) and in German 'Bomheckel', the herb in German being 'bomheckel-krut', adding that it is not good for people generally to know of it as locks fly open before it. The same theme is touched on by Frazer in *The Golden Bough*, who states that in Swabia it was said of a thief who cannot be caught 'he must have springwort'. With it all doors and locks fly open, the bearer of it can become invisible; neither lead nor steel can wound one who carries it in the right hand pocket of his coat.

Similar tales crop up in French folklore, thus:

> The herb of the green woodpecker is a magical plant which has the property of communicating a supernatural force to those who rub their limbs with it.
>
> Here is the means to procure it: observe the flight and the habits of the green woodpecker and when it is seen to stop near a herb on which it rubs its beak, one can flatter oneself that the precious talisman has been found. This incomparable herb which gives the green woodpecker the strength to drill into the bark of the strongest oaks, is also found sometimes in the nest of the same bird. Furthermore, one can be certain that this plant is covered in dew in both summer and winter.

Iron must not be used to pluck or gather it ...

In several of our villages, the poor devils waste their time seeking this treasure and their number should be considerable, if, as it is said, every time that the green woodpecker makes the valleys echo with its prolonged and mocking cry, which resembles a hearty laugh, it is because it sees one of these prowlers seeking its herb.

The springwort legend has been recorded in Wales where it was said that placed in a stick it would offer protection against robbers and could be used to locate iron ore. The reference to a stick is an interesting variation here and is perhaps a confused description of a dowser's divining-rod. The same author states that the woodpecker is associated with Welsh lore and specially acquainted with the magic virtue of herbs, although not specifically relating the bird to the obtaining of springwort.

However, the question remains as to what the point of these stories is. At times they seem fairly practical. Having enlisted the help of the woodpecker to obtain the magic plant, its possessor has a talisman which will open any lock and gives him power or protection, particularly over and against iron objects. Other versions of these tales seem to have a more esoteric content and the pursuit of the magic plant takes on a symbolic and mystical meaning. Folktales of hidden treasure guarded by fairies or dragons are common enough, and in some versions of the springwort legends we seem to be touching on a story which is symbolic of man's deep-seated search for fulfilment and there are echoes of a quest which is reminiscent of the legends of the Holy Grail.

Belief in an enchanted treasure which could only be recoverd under certain conditions was widespread in Teutonic tradition. Donar was the Germanic god of thunder and his thunderbolt was symbolized by an axe. At a later stage this came to be portrayed as a hammer, and small hammer-shaped amulets have been found in the graves of Anglo-Saxons to whom he was known as Thunor, from which our word for thunder and the fifth day of the week, Thursday, are derived. In one of the sagas, Donar's hammer is plunged into the earth from whence it strives to come to the surface, moving it is said, at the rate of a cock's stride each year. The same pattern is followed in other treasure legends; as it rose slowly to the surface the treasure was said to blossom, ripen and then sink back in to the earth. It ripened every seven years, or in some cases only once in a hundred years and then particularly at the time of full moon. In another reference the treasure is said to sun itself on a Friday in March (perhaps Friday as this day was called after Frija, the earth goddess of the Germanic world). In other accounts the treasure does not rise but remains hidden deep in the earth or in a cave.

In one story related by Kuhn in his *North German Legends*, a shepherd who was driving his flock over the Ilsenstein, stopped to rest and was leaning on his staff which unknown to him contained springwort, when the mountainside opened and a princess stood before him. The shepherd was bidden to enter the mountain and help himself to as much gold as he wished. He filled his pockets and started to leave when the princess called to him, 'Forget not the best'. Thinking that her intention was that he should take more, the peasant filled his hat with treasure but in fact she was referring to his staff, containing the springwort, which he had laid against the wall when he entered. Forgetting all about this in his excitement the shepherd started to depart but as he tried to leave the treasure cave, the rocks at the entrance slammed together and he was cut in two.

There are other variants of the story but the constant strands are of a man gaining entrance to a mountain cave through carrying with him, albeit inadvertently, the magic herb and his being invited to help himself to gold by a white lady or other female benefactress who then warns him not to 'forget the best'. This is followed by the man ignoring the herb which has brought him in and his consequent death or maiming as he attempts to leave.

Sometimes the man is said to have found the flower, often blue, which is the springwort and to have put it in his hat. It is the hat which he then puts down to gather the gold, thus sealing his fate when he departs without it. Perhaps the hat here represents his mental faculties and he may thus be said to have 'lost his head' over the gold.

In Swabia, if the plant was buried in the ground at the summit of a mountain, it was said to draw down the lightning and divide the storm to the left and right of it. Rocks and mountains can be taken as synonymous with clouds in folk-lore and therefore the treasure is the rain released by the thunder.

The treasure was only to be obtained by those worthy of it. To raise it, silence was essential and if he who found it cried out it would immediately sink from sight. The other vital requirement was innocence. The harmless hand of childhood is fit to lay hold on it; poor village boys and shepherd lads are they that find it, we are told in the saga of Donar; he that is stained with vice can never come near it.

Another requirement was that iron must not be used in the cutting or gathering of it. There is a link here with mistletoe which was revered by both the Druids and the Italians and both banned the use of iron in gathering it. Both linked its powers to the phases of the moon, although the Druids considered it should be cut on the sixth day after the new moon and the Italians on the first day. Again, as with the moonwort, the mistletoe must not fall to the ground but should be caught in a cloth.

Taboos against iron are very common. Frazer in *The Golden Bough* lists numerous examples: Roman and Sabine priests might not be shaved with iron but only with bronze. No iron tool might be brought into the sacred grove of the Arval Brothers (the priests of Mars) at Rome without sacrifices being offered to expiate the fault. Similar rules applied in Crete and Greece and in modern times a Hottentot priest had to use a sharp splinter of quartz rather than an iron knife in sacrificing an animal. The Jews used no iron tool in building the Temple at Jerusalem or in making an altar. Frazer suggests that this superstitious objection to iron stems from a time when iron was a novelty and was viewed with suspicion but this seems unconvincing. The same objections could have been made to copper or bronze when they were novelties and one would expect the superior qualities of iron for making cutting tools to cause it to be revered rather than the reverse.

It would seem that while men in the iron age and later were highly appreciative of the practical advantages of the new metal, at the same time they were aware of some quality in it which dimmed their own sensitivities in the occult field; this would account for the ban on the use of iron being always confined to the priesthood and the sacred places.

Most of the stories concerning the springwort refer to obtaining access in some way, whether on the mundane level of opening locks fashioned by man or the freeing of a blocked entrance to a nest but also more esoterically, offering the means to enter hidden stores of treasure deep in the earth. It is significant that in all these tales man either finds himself in possession of the springwort by mere chance or else he has to enlist the aid of the woodpecker to find it. What is the faculty which the bird has but which is barred from man's conscious mind?

The bird symbolizes that essence of Nature which runs through all creation and the intuition, now lost or dormant in man, which enabled him to attune himself to the energies which resound throughout all the natural world. On a practical level this could enable him to find sources of water and those places on the surface of the earth where beneficial energies are concentrated. It could also lead him to a greater understanding of his own spiritual existence, for was not the woodpecker also considered to be an oracle and bird of prophecy?

The Cult of the Green Bird

Picus and the Plough

THE GREEN WOODPECKER is often to be seen on the ground, probing the earth with its beak in its search for ants and it is not surprising therefore to find the bird linked with the myths and legends surrounding the first plough and the beginnings of agriculture.

Early man was a nomad and a hunter but at some stage he began to plant crops and harvest them; this called for a suitable climate and permanent habitation in one spot, thus engendering the formation of the first villages and later of towns. The views of historians and archaeologists have been modified as to the question of where this revolution first took place and it is now thought that agriculture originated simultaneously at a number of places along the so called 'fertile crescent', which stretches from Palestine through Mesopotamia to Iran. The village sites showing evidence of early agriculture north of the River Tigris must all have enjoyed a mild climate and were situated in wooded country. Here, about 7,000 BC, we may envisage cereals and vegetables being planted in woodland clearings or around trees deadened by fire or natural causes. The digging necessary before planting could take place would be easier in these locations than in open grassland, where sods would be difficult to turn over and the grasses would tend to overwhelm the crops.

Before the invention of the plough drawn by animals the soil was broken up using simple pointed digging sticks and later it was found that these were more effective when weighted with stones; obviously none of these sticks have survived but the stone weights have been found. The first farmers laboriously tilling the soil in this way at the edge of the woods must have worked in precisely those areas frequented by green woodpeckers, which prefer such places to dense woodland, and the birds' expert delving into the ground in search of food would have seemed a clear parallel to man's own efforts.

As we have seen it is in this same area of the Near East that the first indications of a cult of the green bird can be traced and it is not difficult to see how it became associated with fertility and husbandry in this way. The next link between the woodpecker and the plough is to be found among the myths of ancient Greece. Celeus, whose name means green woodpecker was a king of Eleusis, whose eldest son was Triptolemus. Demeter, the corn goddess, while wandering in the disguise of an old woman was befriended by Metaneira, the wife of Celeus and lived for a time in his palace. Having revealed herself she gave Triptolemus a grain of corn and showed him how to plough with oxen. Conveniently supplied with a winged chariot drawn by dragons he travelled throughout Greece and beyond, teaching people wherever he went how to plough and grow corn. Finally he returned to Eleusis, was protected by Demeter from the wrath of Celeus and then took over the throne from him.

It seems clear that this tale is allegorical; Celeus, the woodpecker, represents man's first simple attempts at agriculture using the digging stick technique so similar to the probing of the green bird; to this day we call such an instrument a pick, a word derived from the same root as Picus. In due course the pick had to give way to the plough drawn by animals.

A similar theme is taken up in a much later tale, recorded from among the Lettish population in what is now Poland. According to this story God and the Devil each had a field to plough, the Devil using horses to draw his plough while God used a woodpecker. At the end of the day the Devil had ploughed a large area but God had covered very little ground, so during the night he took the Devil's horses and finished ploughing his field. When the Devil saw this in the morning he was most impressed and asked if he could exchange his horses for the woodpecker, which he thought would be less trouble to feed. The exchange was made but the woodpecker, having been harnessed, could not stir the plough. In a rage the Devil struck at the bird and broke his head and thus the woodpecker's head is red to this day.

For the peoples who first practised agriculture, the seasons of sowing and of harvest must have been all-important. At harvest time not only were the crops gathered in to give food for the winter but at this time the seed corn had to be set aside to ensure the next year's harvest and the animals divided up into those to be kept to maintain the breeding stock and those to be slaughtered for food.

Little has come down to us regarding the festivals of these first farmers but we can be sure that the harvest would have been an outstanding date in their calendar, as it has been with all primitive people who till the soil. This season, linked to the cycles of the moon, has always been a time of celebration for them and a moment to pause and look forward to the next spring and plan for the continued well being of the community. A great gathering would be required to celebrate the success of the harvest and for the elders of the tribe to proclaim plans for the new season.

At such times as these we know that the Red Indian tribes would assemble around their ceremonial fires and conjure up visions of their spirit guides, soaring eagles or strong bears. Those who took the woodpecker as their guide must have done the same. The Dene Indians of north-western Canada had a tradition that the thunder bird was so large that it darkened the heavens. Perhaps there is a folk echo here of a time when a vision of the archetypal guide of a tribe was shown to all who were present. Sensitives, able to delve back into the distant past, have described such gatherings in sacred groves with the oversoul of the great woodpecker, a huge apparition with outstretched wings, visible to all, hovering above the assembled tribe.

Man still had a respect for all his companions on the planet and for the earth itself. Nature was a power to be respected, a bountiful provider of all his needs, in

The Cult of the Green Bird

harmony with the sun and firmament above. Over all the Sky God was the power behind the visible sun. Amongst the planets, Mars, the thrusting life force, coupled with the creative power of Venus, gave life and fertility to all living things.

The Cult of the Green Bird

The Bee-Wolf

APART FROM HIS SKILL AS A PLOUGHMAN, the woodpecker has other abilities which man could envy and attempt to emulate. Honey was an invaluable natural sweetener and source of nourishment, thought to be the food of the gods and highly prized, so much so that a land 'flowing with milk and honey' was the way in which the Israelites described their cherished goal when seeking to escape from their enslavement in Egypt. The classical writers of Rome looked back to the mythical days when Saturn (father of Picus) ruled over a land where the fruits of the field and honey were plentiful for all. These images must relate back to a time before bees had been domesticated and the precious honey had to be gathered from the nests of wild bees. Here the woodpecker must have been regarded as both a rival and a model; bees nest naturally in hollow trees and the green woodpecker's habit of searching these out and braving the bees' wrath to get at their larvae and the honey would be well-known. The ease with which the woodpecker could alight on a tree near a bees' nest or climb up to it, extract the prize with its strong bill and then make a rapid withdrawal, must have been much envied. There are echoes of this respect for the bird's skill in a statement by Pliny, writing at a later date, when bees had become domesticated, that a beekeeper should carry a woodpecker's beak when taking honey from a hive in order to avoid being stung.

In Germany the bird's reputation gave it the name of Beowolf (the bee-wolf), a fitting name for one who actively seeks out the bees. This habit has caused some trouble in modern times as it was found that it was for this reason that green woodpeckers attacked telegraph poles, boring deep cavities in the wood in pursuit of what they imagined to be wild bees' nests. At first it was considered that these onslaughts were simply carried out in search of any sort of food or to provide nest holes. The Post Office, then responsible for the nation's telephone network, most of which was carried by overhead lines, started routine checks for this sort of damage as far back as 1932. The holes which were found were filled in with various substances, including concrete, but it was soon found that some poles were attacked more frequently than others and it was suggested that the humming of the wires led the birds to believe that bees' nests were hidden in the wood. Experiments showed that if the familiar humming noise was supressed by wrapping strips of lead around the insulators, the woodpeckers lost interest.

The difficulties and dangers of obtaining honey from wild bees must have turned man's mind quite early to the possibility of taming these useful but rather fearsome creatures so that a supply of the much sought after honey could be assured and obtained with less danger.

The people of Mesopotamia did not keep bees in hives until a late date but the Egyptians practised this art early in their history. In Roman times when Virgil came to write the *Georgics* he devoted the whole of one of its four books to 'the celestial gift of honey' and the craft of beekeeping.

In Greek mythology it was Aristaeus (whose name simply means 'the very good') who took bees from the oak trees and taught men how to make beehives. Different parts of Greece had their own gods who fulfilled the functions of Pan and in Thessaly it was Aristaeus who was the guardian of flocks and took this part. He was sometimes known as Aristaeus Zeus and became confused with Zeus himself; this leads us on to another story concerned with honey.

Antonius Liberalis reported a Cretan tradition in relation to the birth cave of Zeus. It was said that Celeus, whose name means green woodpecker in Greek and whom we have already met in the guise of the father of Triptolemus, visited the cave with some companions seeking to steal the honey from the sacred bees, whose task it was to feed the infant god. They had protected themselves with bronze armour but when they looked on Zeus' swaddling clothes, the bronze shattered: the gods would have killed them but Themis and the Fates intervened saying that blood must not be spilt in such a holy place, so Zeus turned all the malefactors into a number of different birds which thereafter were considered to give the most reliable omens and amongst these Celeus himself became a green woodpecker.

The Cult of the Green Bird

Given that the green woodpecker's fondness for honey was well-known, it remains to be explained why he has been cast in the role of a thief and why he is in competition with Zeus. The story is set in Crete where images of a bee-headed goddess were common and it was anciently believed that bees were begotten of bulls, arising from the dead carcass of the animal; they were thus a symbol of regeneration. Bees were associated with oak trees, probably because their nests would be found in these trees more than any other. Oaks being long-lived trees, these were more likely to contain the hollow spaces which the bees needed for nesting. The woodpecker was also associated with the oak and there was another link in that the woodpecker and bees were connected with thunder.

Thus we have the woodpecker who took his part in the annual rebirth of the spirits of regrowth and fertility replaced by Zeus, the more anthropomorphic god but with rejuvenation still symbolized by the bees. According to Rendel Harris, the point of the tale is that old thunder (the woodpecker) is deposed by the new. Zeus takes the sceptre and occupies a cave instead of a woodland sanctuary, while the bees, symbols of rebirth, accompany him. As in many myths the real meaning has been inverted; it is Zeus who 'steals' from the woodpecker Picus or Celeus, rather than the other way round.

Once the idea of keeping bees in artificial hives was established, the need to attract a swarm to the new hive by making as much noise as possible was soon learned and is still practised by banging metal pans together or any similar means of making such a crude sound. In the *Georgics* Virgil shows that this was well known in his day and refers to the need to clash cymbals:

> Tinnitusque cie et Matris quate cymbala circum
> Ipsae ceriscden medicates sedibus

(i.e make a tinkling sound and clash the Great Mother's cymbals around: they (the bees) will settle on the scented place of their own accord.)
A little later in the same poem he describes the feeding of the infant Zeus in the Dictaean cave by the bees summoned by the clashing of the bronze shields of the Corybantes, who were there to guard the god. Here Virgil seems to equate the Corybantes with the Curetes. Thus the story of the birth cave of Zeus may also be a description of the domestication of bees, moved from their natural nests in hollow trees into a man-made structure.

The Woodpecker in Literature

IN PREVIOUS CHAPTERS reference has been made to works on mythology and folklore in which the woodpecker has figured but this bird has also found a place in more general literature describing its habits and the way in which it has enriched the rural scene.

In English literature, apart from a doubtful reference to the green woodpecker in the Exeter Book of Anglo-Saxon Riddles, we have to look to the thirteenth and fourteenth centuries to find it recorded. John of Guildford in his poem 'The Owl and the Nightingale', written about 1225, refers to the wudewall and Chaucer in 'The Romaunt and The Rose' (1369) uses the same name but neither of these poems contain any description of the bird.

Michael Drayton (1563–1631) in his poem 'The Owl' describes how this bird of the night was persecuted by the other birds:

> The woodpecker, whose hardened beak has broke,
> And pierc'd the heart of many a solid oak;
>
> The crow is digging at his breast amain;
> And sharp-neb'd hecco stabbing at his brain.

In another poem, 'A Warwickshire Morning' he gives a fine description of a landscape at dawn resonant with a chorus of birds including 'the laughing hecco'.

None of these authors do much more than mention the woodpecker, using various local names, amongst a catalogue of birds and we must move on to the seventeenth century and Andrew Marvell's poem 'Upon Appleton House, to My Lord Fairfax' to find a real description of the yaffle in its own environment. Marvell, a colleague of Milton, was living on the Yorkshire estate of Lord Fairfax, the commander-in-chief of the parliamentary forces during the first stage of the Civil War when the poem was written. It is a long work in which he imagines himself wandering into the woods where he is gradually enfolded by its green kingdom. After describing various birds he continues:

> But most the Hewel's* wonders are,
> Who here has the Holt-felsters† care.
> He walks still upright from the Root,
> Meas'ring the Timber with his Foot;
> And all the way, to keep it clean,
> Doth from the Bark the Wood-moths glean.
> He, with his Beak, examines well
> Which fit to stand and which to fell.
>
> The good he numbers up, and hacks;
> As if he mark'd them with the Ax.
> But where he, tinkling with his Beak,
> Does find the hollow Oak to speak,
> That for his building he designs,
> And through the tainted Side he mines.
> Who could have thought the tallest Oak
> Should fall by such a feeble Strok'!

Nor would it, had the Tree not fed
A Traitor-worm within it bred.
(As first our Flesh corrupt within
Tempts impotent and bashful Sin.)
And yet that Worm triumphs not long,
But serves to feed the Hewel's young.
While the Oake seems to fall content,
Viewing the Treason's Punishement.

* the green woodpecker
† woodcutters.

Clearly Andrew Marvell was familiar with the behaviour of the green woodpecker and must have watched these birds work their way methodically up trees in the upright position which he describes, pausing to drill into the rotten timber from time to time to find their food.

In the eighteenth century Gilbert White was a meticulous observer of all facets of natural history; his famous letters, published as *The Natural History of Selborne*, contain only short references to the woodpecker's undulating flight and call but the bird also figures in several entries in his Journals. These were written in White's unique laconic style and have the knack of setting a scene with a minimum of words; thus his entry for April 16th, 1770 reads: 'Green Woodpecker laughs at all the world', which seems to say it all.

In the next century Richard Jefferies does not seem to have written much about the woodpecker in his books but he was obviously well-acquainted with it in Wiltshire, as shown by a letter he wrote to *The Swindon Advertiser* in 1871:

The Cult of the Green Bird

90 – *The Woodpecker in Literature*

The woodpecker; the gamekeepers say this bird is scarce but it is not. Any attentive observer will frequently hear its wild eldritch chuckle, like sardonic laughter. The old Wiltshire name was yuckle, a word which represents the sound made by the bird.

> Just then a yuckle passing by
> Was asked by them the cause to try. (Old Ballard)

Later, when living in Sussex Jefferies does include a description of the woodpecker in his essay 'Nature near Brighton':

> A green woodpecker starts from a tree, and can be watched between the trunks as he flies; his bright colour marks him. Presently, on rounding some furze, he rises again, this time from the ground, and goes over the open glade; flying the green woodpecker appears a larger bird than would be supposed if seen when still. He has been among the beeches all the time, and it was his 'Yuc, yuc' which we heard. Where the woodpecker is heard and seen, there the woods are woods and wild - a sense of wildness accompanies his presence.

A less well known author, J. A. Owen in *Forest Tithes* (1893) describes the cheerful antics of a woodpecker on some fallen trees:

> On their grey trunks the yaffle shins about, yells, laughs and yikes to his heart's content. Now and again he pokes his head over the side of a limb as he clings to the bark, makes a dive off to the next tree, taps and peeps again.

In the twentieth century W. H. Hudson did much to make people more aware of the wild life that surrounded them and he took a leading part in the foundation of the Royal Society for the Protection of Birds. In *Birds and Man* he wrote of his visit to the small city of Wells in Somerset:

> But it is hard to imagine a birdless Wells. The hills, beautiful with trees and grass and flowers, come down to it; cattle graze on their slopes; the peewit has its nest in their stony places, and the kestrel with quick-beating wings hangs motionless overhead. Nature is round it, breathing upon and touching it caressingly on every side; flowing through it like the waters that gave it its name in olden days, that still gush with noise and foam from the everlasting rock, to send their crystal currents along the streets. And with nature, in and around the rustic village-like city live the birds. The green woodpecker laughs aloud from the group of old cedars and pines, hard by the cathedral close – you will not hear that woodland sound in any other city in the kingdom.

The green woodpecker is well described in Wilfred Willett's *British Birds*, published in 1948:

> The bird flies across the meadow with a bounding switch-back flight, using its wings on the downward flight and closing them on the upward curve. You notice the short tail. Often as it flies the laughing call is uttered. This jolly laugh is one of the pleasant sounds of the countryside. I have heard it every month of the year, but I like to hear it most in the autumn when the oak

leaves are browning, and yellow and crimson cherry leaves are falling as the wind sweeps by, turning and twisting them; and as the sun shines out at the edge of ragged clouds, then the Galleybird laughs with seeming joy.

A final excerpt comes from an essay, 'The Awakener of the Woods' by Fiona Macleod. This name was a pseudonym of William Sharp, a mystic and author who wrote largely of the Western Isles of Scotland and their Celtic traditions and folklore but whose work also covered a wider spectrum. He was clearly fascinated by the green woodpecker and the mythology surrounding it and the following is a small part of the beautiful essay which he wrote about the bird:

> It was in the Forest of Fontainebleau I first heard the green woodpecker called by this delightful name, the Awakener of the Woods, le Réveilleur de la Forêt. My French friend told me it was not a literary name, as I fancied, but one given by the foresters. And how apt it is. In the first weeks of March – in the first week of April, it may be, as the scene moves northward – there is no more delightful, and certainly no more welcome, sound than the blithe bugle-call of the green woodpecker calling through the woods for love, and, after long expectant pauses, hearing love call back in thrilling response, now a flute-note of gladness, now a challenging clarion-cry. True, whether in the vast forest of Fontainebleau or in our northern woods the woodpecker is not so readily to be heard in the inward solitudes. He loves the open glades, and commonly the timbered park-land

is his favourite resort. Still, save in the deepest and darkest woods, that delightful rejoicing note is now everywhere to be heard fluting along the sunlit ways of the wind. It awakes the forest. When the voice of the woodpecker is heard it is the hour for Nature to celebrate her own Ides of March. Elsewhere the song-thrush and the skylark have been the first heralds. Even in the woods the missel-thrush may have flung a sudden storm of song out on the cold tides of the wind swaying the elm-tops like dusky airweed of the upper ocean. But, in the glades themselves, in the listening coverts, it is the call of the green woodpecker that has awakened the dreaming forest.

The Cult of the Green Bird

Bestiaries and Emblems

BESTIARIES AND EMBLEMS may be regarded as a separate branch of literature since they were works of reference with a definite purpose in a narrow field. In the middle ages bestiaries became popular as works which not only described the wonders of the animal kingom but pointed out the moral lessons which each species was supposed to offer to mankind. These 'books of beasts' contained information handed down from classical authors such as Heroditus, Aristotle and Pliny. Sometime between the 2nd and 5th centuries AD they were collated into the most famous source for medieval bestiaries, the *Physiologus*, by an unknown writer, probably in Egypt. It was translated from the original Greek into many languages, the earliest surviving Latin edition dating from the 8th century. The information it contained, both on mythical beasts and more recognizable species of animal was copied into many works and elaborated upon by Christian writers who were not content merely to describe the wonders of creation. They considered that every species held out an object lesson to mankind, either as an example of good behaviour or as a warning to the potential sinner. The habits of each of the Lord's creatures were thus to be studied, not simply to gain knowledge of natural history but as symbols of moral qualities, good or bad, provided by God for man's guidance.

The woodpecker received rather a mixed press in these bestiaries and the emblems (or parables) which were popular well into the 17th century. According to the *Physiologus* the brightly coloured woodpecker symbolized the Devil, full of craft, who seeks out the sinner in the same way as the woodpecker seeks out a rotten tree in which to make its nest. *Narrenschiff* (The Ship of Fools) by Sebastian Brant, published in 1494 includes an engraving showing a man in fool's costume with a woodpecker tapping in a tree nearby. The moral is to avoid idle talk:

> Who guards his speech and holds his tongue
> By anguish ne'er his soul is stung;
> Woodpeckers' screech betrays their young.

Jacob Cats, a Dutch lawyer and poet, thought the woodpecker had too high an opinion of itself and attempted tasks which were beyond its capabilities:

> The woodpecker flutters everywhere, sweeps through the thickets and hedges; it seems as though he wants to declare war on the trees. He pecks into every kind of wood and he looks for an open space. But the bark hardly smells his breath.

Thus, said Cats, people have an exaggerated opinion of their own powers. However the symbolism of the woodpecker was not always cast on the negative side. According to Picinelli the bird was to be likened to a studious man and 'latentia tentat' (he seeks hidden things) is given as the rubric. Camerarius in his emblem wrote;

> Spernit humum picus, petit ardua sic quoque virtus
> Appetit excelsis sacra reposta locis.

In other words, as the woodpecker scorns the earth and makes for the heights, so does virtue seek sacred things stored in high places.

Conclusion

IN PREVIOUS CHAPTERS we have traced the progress of the green bird during some eight thousand years from the time when he was an early god of agriculture and fertility in his own right, through stages as a representative of Mars and an oracular creature, to his becoming the rain bird and weather prophet in much European folklore.

Why should man have worshipped birds? They have an appeal not only to the eye, as have many other creatures, but to the ear as well and in their songs and courtship rituals, their nest-building and care for their young, they can invoke an emotional response to which man can relate directly; and yet they are of another world and are free to move in another element. What could be more natural than to deify them?

Gilbert Murray in his introduction to Aristophanes' *Birds* wrote:

> There is a tradition, he might remember, that our ancestors had other gods before these anthropomorphic Olympians were introduced; sometimes, it may be, they worshipped birds; how much more sensible! The Birds ask for so little and have so much to give. They want

no great temples or sacrifices; they insist on no long pilgrimages before they will speak to us. They are here, living, flying and singing among us; we can see the joy that is in their hearts, joy that we creatures of clay can never reach. Yet if we worshipped them rightly, who knows?, they might let us have some share in it.

Early religions, whatever their particular variations, all tended to recognize man's need for a harmonious relationship with nature. The concept of a Great Goddess, or Mother Goddess, lasted from the neolithic age right through to Minoan times. At first we find her portrayed as a pregnant female figure and the emphasis appears to have been on fertility, the life cycle and death; figurines of the Great Goddess occur in large numbers in tombs, showing a belief in some form of rebirth and perhaps of reincarnation. After the coming of agriculture there was a tendency for the goddess to become the Earth Mother, often indistinguishable from the Earth itself. As such she was associated with a male consort, son, brother or husband, a vegetation god who died and was reborn each spring. In this manner the death of Tammuz, the beloved of the goddess Ishtar, was celebrated each autumn in Mesopotamia over hundreds of years. The worship of the Great Goddess spread in due course to Crete and from thence to Myceneian Greece. It was a Greek tradition that looked back to the time of the early gods when Picus the woodpecker ruled before Zeus the anthropomorphic god took over the sceptre.

In Italy it was Mars, the god who represented male energy and gave his name to the month of the year which saw new life springing up, who was the principal agricultural god and we have seen the ambiguous role of the woodpecker as his symbol and also as a minor god of the mountains and forests in its own right.

Gradually the worship of earth and sky, once carried out in the open air, perhaps at a simple altar of turf or beside a sacred spring, became constrained into city temples each occupied by its own anthropomorphic god. However, it was not until the Christian Church became the dominant political power of the Roman Empire that the link with the natural forces of the earth was broken. Christianity was built on the bedrock of the Hebrew religion which recognized a single male deity, a 'jealous God' who would brook no tolerance towards other beliefs. In the early Church every vestige of paganism had to be stamped out. The power of local heathen holy places and their hold over the local population was recognized however, and had to be adapted to the Church's purposes. The instructions of Pope Gregory the Great to St Augustine, as recorded by Bede, in this context are well known: The heathen temples found in England were not to be destroyed, rather they were to be purified by smashing any idols found therein and sprinkling the actual temples with holy water, after which they could be rededicated. In this way it was hoped that the people, by continuing to frequent their former places of worship, would turn more easily to the true God.

It was a prime objective of the Church to consign all the old religions to oblivion and so far as written records were concerned, it was largely successful, since churchmen alone normally had the ability to read and write.

6. Woodpeckers depicted on a carved bench end in Trull Church, Somerset.

(16th century)

Photograph: *Author's private collection.*

Our knowledge of the religion which was practised by our ancestors before their conversion to Christianity is thus very limited. However the spoken word and the desire of ordinary people to cling to the beliefs of their forefathers was a different matter and Church edicts issued from time to time are clear evidence that some of the old ways survived. Archbishop Theodore's Penitential in the seventh century forbade idolatry, the worship of wells, trees, stones etc., and the practice of astrology, augury and divination. Three hundred years later King Cnut was still having to issue similar prohibitions, so it is obvious that an undercurrent of the old pagan ways still existed. Place names, too, often reveal the old cult centres of heathen gods, such as Woden, whose name has been incorporated into places as far afield as Kent and Derbyshire, and the Vale of Pewsey in Wiltshire has several such names, including Wansdyke (or Woden's dic) the great ditch which runs for miles across the downs.

In the teaching of the Church all the pagan gods became devils and the Evil One himself was portrayed with horns on his head and cloven hooves, precisely the features attributed to Pan and the nature gods of old. Pan was said to have been born from a woodpecker's egg and Faunus, in classical mythology was the son of Picus. In medieval times the woodpecker was allowed to maintain a place in folklore but it is significant that in tales which have been overlaid with a Christian theme the bird is cast in the role of the villain or alternatively, the villain is transformed into a woodpecker as a punishment. Thus, alone of all the birds, the woodpecker was said to have disobeyed God's command to dig out the seas and in a Welsh story, Christ curses an old woman who refused him food and turns her into a woodpecker. These and other folk tales seem to show that there was felt to be a need to demonstrate that the bird, an archetype of the forces of nature, had been banished from its former position.

In view of this determination to stifle the old religions, it is all the more surprising to find two figures appearing in church sculptures from the eleventh century onwards which relate back to the Great Earth Mother. In many parts of Europe, particularly at sites formerly associated with the Earth Mother or with Isis, statues of the Black Virgin appeared. The image of the Virgin with the Christ child may well hark back to the Egyptian worship of Isis and the child Horus or it may simply have been a spontaneous solution to the need for the feminine principle to be acknowledged in some way in the otherwise male-dominated tenets of Christianity. During the same period, carvings of the 'Green Man', a figure entwined with vegetation which was usually shown as coming out of the figure's mouth, became common decorative features in church architecture. William Anderson in his book *Green Man* which gives a detailed history of this symbol of man's link with nature, shows how these figures were often put in close proximity to those of the Virgin, as if looking back to the Earth Mother or to Isis and her dead lover, reborn each year.

It is fortunate that during the period in which the Church dominated men's lives and was the final arbiter of most people's thinking, some faint remnants of man's belief in his fundamental involvement with Nature were retained. However, by the eighteenth century new ideas were coming to the fore. The arguments now were not between Catholic and Protestant; the established Churches in most countries had lapsed into a religious torpor, bastions of privilege for a priesthood mainly concerned with its own power and possessions. In France this was swept aside by the Revolution. In England it was said that religion was dead and if anyone mentioned religion there, people began to laugh.

The Age of Reason had replaced the Age of Faith. Newton appeared to have unlocked the secrets of the universe and a new atmosphere of scientific enquiry sought to explain all the wonders of creation. Man, it was stated in the book of Genesis, had been given dominion over every living thing that moved upon the earth and he now set out to examine and catalogue all these wonders. This was at a time when the European nations were expanding their horizons as never before in search of wealth and power in new lands and this often involved exploiting all the living creatures which they found there, including the native populations. From Australia to North America the white man imposed his culture and his rule and when in the nineteenth century a revival in Christianity led to a new missionary zeal, the conversion of the indigenous peoples of the new colonies was carried out with no allowance for the former beliefs of the inhabitants. There is no doubt that many men and women dedicated their lives to enhancing the spiritual and physical well-being of the native populations but there was a regrettable contempt for ancient cultures: the words of Bishop Heber's well-known hymn typifies this attitude:

> In vain with lavish kindness
> The gifts of God are strown;
> The heathen in his blindness
> Bows down to wood and stone.

The wood and stone which the heathen bowed down to were symbols of the native's spirit gods and the bishop seems to have ignored the fact that many Christians bowed to images of their own!

What was lacking was the recognition of a need for harmony and a mutual respect between all living creatures and consideration for the earth itself as a living entity. This was the creed of the North American Indians and other aboriginal peoples, as discussed in an earlier chapter.

In Europe nevertheless, alongside the ambiguous attitudes of a new interest in nature, coupled with its ruthless exploitation, there was a move among philosophers and poets towards what has been described as the worship of Nature but perhaps could more accurately be termed worship through Nature. The natural landscape was not generally appreciated by the medieval mind and wild mountain scenery, cascading waterfalls or lonely woods were viewed merely as a hazard to travellers, along with wild beasts and robbers. Poets such as James Thomson began to write about the beauty of the natural world in the eighteenth century but it was Rousseau and later Goethe who brought a mystical element to its contemplation.

Rousseau wrote: 'In my room I pray less often and with less fervour; but at the sight of a beautiful landscape I feel moved, although I cannot say by what.' And in another passage: 'I can think of no more fitting homage to the Divinity than the silent wonder aroused by the contemplation of His works' and he describes how in watching the waves on the waters of the Lake of Bienne, he lost all sense of his individual identity and became at one with Nature. It was Blake however, who expressed a feeling of responsibility and compassion for our fellow creatures, lacking since the preaching of St Francis and who recognized the essential unity of all nature, writing:

> Everything that lives
> Lives not alone, nor for itself.

and

> Kill not the moth nor butterfly
> For the Last Judgement draweth nigh.

Wordsworth and Coleridge continued the theme and the latter's 'Rime of the Ancient Mariner', with its story of the slaying of the Albatross, the bird of 'good omen', in breach of the laws of hospitality, may be seen as an allegory of man's loss of faith with Nature and his destruction of other inhabitants of this planet, which leads to the unleashing of malevolent forces outside his control. At the end of the poem the Mariner admonished:

> He prayeth well, who loveth well
> Both man and bird and beast.
> He prayeth best, who loveth best

All things both great and small;
For the dear God who loveth us,
He made and loveth all.

Thus a sense of responsibility for man's conduct towards the multitude of living things around him and to the earth was gradually reawakened and in the next century there came a renewed interest in mythology and mysticism and on a more mundane level, in the folklore of different nations.

Man's psyche also became a subject of reserach and the work of Carl Jung did much to clarify the inner recesses of the conscious and subconscious mind. His theories of archetypes and synchronicity strike similar chords to the Stoics' concept of 'universal matter' by which they explained divination through studying such things as the stars and the behaviour of birds.

In these ways there came a new realization of the validity of much from the past which had come to be considered either false or made up from childish fantasies. In the second half of the twentieth century the 'green movement' gathered strength; the study of dowsing, earth energies and similar phenomena has become widespread, while societies and pressure groups campaigning for the preservation of wild life and the earth's natural resources have flourished. At the same time, man's ability to destroy the environment has increased immeasurably; modern technology can literally move mountains and the demands of a rapacious materialistic society are not only becoming greater but are spreading inevitably to the so-called undeveloped countries. The conflict between the aims of conservation and ruthless destruction is inevitable and the outcome can only be contemplated with hope rather than confidence.

What then of the woodpecker? The bird has figured in man's religion, in his struggles to till the soil, to look into his future and to know the will of his gods. To some he has been an oracle, guardian of mystical treasures holding knowledge of destructive thunder and life-giving rain. Associated with the cult of twins he is of Gemini, linked with Venus and Mars; a bird who is at home clinging to the trunks of trees but unlike other woodpeckers, spends much time on the ground. He cannot soar like an eagle but his ways are associated more with the skills which mankind has sought to acquire as ploughman and carpenter. His cry is half human so that it is called a laugh and yet it is of another world.

An archetype of Nature, he reminds us of where we have come from and the need to return to our roots if the planet is to be saved. When W. H. Hudson revisited the city of Wells after an absence of ten years, he heard the call of the green woodpecker as on his previous visit and took its laugh as an assurance that Nature had suffered no change. One could not say that today, but where the yaffle is heard there is always beauty, whether it is on open downland, in green meadows or in woods of oak, ash and beech and his call still reminds us that Pan may seem to sleep but is not dead.

Folk Names of the Green Woodpecker

A LARGE NUMBER OF local or folk names have been given to the green woodpecker. Sometimes it is difficult to distinguish between those used for the green and those for the other species.

The poem 'The Owl and the Nightingale', written by John of Guildford in the early thirteenth century refers to the green woodpecker as the Wude-wale, which is thought to have come down from the Anglo-Saxon name of 'Hyghwhele'. So too the Anglo-Saxon word 'gal' meaning merry has probably given us the name Galleybird for the laughing green woodpecker, who does indeed seem merry; this seems a more convincing derivation than the alternative explanation, sometimes given, that the name comes from the typical upright stance of the bird on a tree trunk which is remniscent of a carved ship's figurehead.

Most of the names refer either to the bird's call or to its reputation as a weather prophet with variants such as Rain Bird, Storm Cock. There are also references to its habit of boring into trees: thus Awlbird and Whetile, meaning cutter.

The Cult of the Green Bird

In Wales it is recorded as Tyllwr-y-coed (wood borer) as well as the more straight forward Cnocell-y-coed (woodpecker) or simply Cnocell (pecker).

In France the name of Plieu (rain) not only refers to the bird's reputation as a foreteller of rain but imitates the bird's call as 'plieu plieu plieu'. In Germany it was known as 'Giessvogel' (pouring rain bird) and also 'Waldpferd' (wood horse) and 'Wieherspecht' (neighing woodpecker), both derived from its call which was thought to imitate the neighing of a horse.

The following list gives many of the local names of the green woodpecker, listed under the old counties of England, together with those in more general use in England as a whole.

CHESHIRE:	Ettwall.
CORNWALL:	Awl-bird, Kazek, Coit.
DEVONSHIRE:	Woodwall.
ESSEX:	Whetile.
GLOUCESTERSHIRE:	Hakel, Woodsprite, Laughing Betsy, Yuckel.
HAMPSHIRE:	Wood-knacker, Wood Sucker, Yaffler, Yaffingale.
HEREFORESHIRE:	Hickel, Yaffler.
HERTFORDSHIRE:	Whetile.
LEICESTERSHIRE:	Rine Tabberer, Tapperer.
LINCOLNSHIRE:	Woodhack, Greenpeek.
NORFOLK:	Woodsprite, Wood Spack.
NORTHAMPTONSHIRE:	Hickel, Jar Peg, Jack Ickle.
NORTHUMBERLAND:	Pick-A-Tree.
NOTTINGHAMSHIRE:	Nicker-Pecker, Nickle.
OXFORDSHIRE:	Hickel, Eakle, Eccle.

SHROPSHIRE:	Woodchuck, Laughing Bird, Yockle, Ecall, High Hoe.
SOMERSET:	Hew Hole, Wood-pie, Yappingale, Wet Bird.
STAFFORDSHIRE:	Stock Eikle.
SUFFOLK:	Sprite, Wood Spack, Wood Yaffle.
SUSSEX:	Rain Bird, Weather Hatcher.
WARWICKSHIRE:	Hickel.
WILTSHIRE:	Yaffingale, Yuckel.
WORCESTERSHIRE:	Eckle, Stock-eikle, Jack Eikle.
YORKSHIRE:	Hufil.
ENGLAND GENERAL:	Awlbird, Cut-bill, Duffly-Dow, Fina, Galleybird, Hecco, Pick, Popinjay, Rain Bird, Rain Fowl, Speke, Speight, Spick Snapper, Storm Cock, Stock Hekle, Weather Cock, Wele, Wood Pale, Woodall, Woodwale, Yaffle, Yappingale.

Bibliography

Anderson, W., *Green Man*, London, 1990.
Armstrong, E.A., *The Folklore of Birds*, London, 1958.
Aubrey, J., *The Natural History of Wiltshire*, ed. J. Britton, 1847.
Bailey, C., *Phases in the Religion of Ancient Rome*, Oxford, 1932.
Blake, W., *Auguries of Innocence: The Book of Thel.*
Brown, W.J., *The Gods had Wings*, London, 1936.
Carter, J.B., *The Religion of Numa*, London, 1906.
Cary, M. & Scullard, H.H., *A History of Rome*, London, 1935.
Coleridge, S.T. *Poetical Works of*, ed. E.H. Coleridge, Oxford, 1912.
Cook, A.B., *Zeus – a Study in Ancient Religion*, 3 vols, Cambridge, 1914–40.
Culpeper, N., *Complete Herbal and English Physician*, 1826 edn.
Dumézil, G., *Le Festin d'immortalité*, Paris, 1924.
de Fournival, *La Bestiare d'amour*, Paris, 1860.
Frazer, J.G., *The Golden Bough*, London, 1932/35.
Gerard, J., *The Herball*, 2nd edn, 1633.
Gimbutas, M., *The Goddesses and Gods of Old Europe*, London, 1974.
Grimm, J., *Teutonic Mythology*, Berlin, 1875/78.
Halliday, W.R., *Lectures on the History of Roman Religion*, Liverpool, 1932.
———, *Greek Divination*, London, 1913.
Harris, J.R., *Boanerges*, Cambridge, 1913.
———, *Picus who is also Zeus*, Cambridge, 1916.
Harrison, J.E., *Themis – A Study of Social Origins of Greek Religion*, Cambridge, 1912.
Henig, M., *Religion in Roman Britain*, London, 1984.
Hudson, W.H., *Birds and Man*, London, 1901.
———, *Afoot in England*, London, 1909.

Jackson, C., *British Names of Birds*, 1968.
Jefferies, R., *The Life of the Fields*, London, 1884.
——, *Letter to The Swindon Advertiser*, Swindon, 1871.
de Kay, C., *Bird Gods*, New York, 1898.
Kelly, W.K., *Curiosities of Indo-European Tradition & Folklore*, London, 1863.
Lawson, J.C., *Modern Greek Folklore and Ancient Greek Religion*, Cambridge 1910.
Lloyd, L., *Scandinavian Adventures*, 1854.
Mellersh, H.E.L., *The Story of Man*, London, 1959.
——, *From Ape Man to Homer*, London, 1962.
Montgomery, J., *Poetical Works of*, London, 1850.
Murray, A.S., *Manual of Mythology*, London, 1873.
Murray, G.M., *Forward to Aristophanes' The Birds*, London, 1950.
Ogilvie, *The Romans and Their Gods*, London, 1969.
Owen, E., *Welsh Folklore*, Oswestry, 1897.
Owen, J.A., *Forest Tithes*, 1893.
Parke, H.W., *Oracles of Zeus*, Oxford, 1967.
Phipson, E., *The Animal Lore of Shakespeare's Time*, 1883.
Rolland, E., *Faune Populaire de France*, Paris, 1877/83.
Rose, H.J., *Ancient Greek Religion*, London, 1946.
——, *Primitive Culture in Italy*, London, 1926.
Rousseau, J.J., *The Confessions*, 1781.
Roux, G., *Ancient Iraq*, London, 1964.
Rowland, B., *Birds with Human Souls*, Knoxville, 1978.
Salmon, E.T., *Samnium and the Samnites*, Cambridge, 1967.
Scullard, H.H., *A History of The Roman World 753–146 BC*, London, 1935.
Sharpe, W. (Fiona Macleod), *Where the Forest Murmurs*, London, 1910.
Smith, A.C., *The Bird of Wilts*, London, 1887.
Swainson, C., *Provincial Names and Folklore of British Birds*, London, 1885.
Swann, H.K., *Dictionary of English & Folk Names of British Birds*, London, 1913.
Thompson, d'A., *Glossary of Greek Birds*, Oxford, 1936.
Trevelyan, M., *Folklore of Wales*, London, 1909.
White, G., *The Natural History of Selborne*, 1789.
——, *The Journals of Gilbert White*, ed. W. Johnson, London, 1931.

Willett, W., *British Birds*, London, 1948.

Classical Sources

Aristophanes: *The Birds*.
Aristotle: *Historia Animalium*.
Cicero: *De Divinatione I and II*.
Dionysius of Halicarnassus: *Roman Antiquities*.
Ovid: *Fasti I and III*.
———, *Metamorphoses XIV*.
———, *Amores III*.
Pliny: *Natural History*.
Strabo: *Geography IV*.
Virgil: *Aeneid VII*.
———, *Georgics IV*.

Index

Adriatic 23–6
Aeneas 29, 30
Africa 65
agriculture, birth of 63, 78
ancilia 35
Anderson, William 103
Anglesey 39
Anglo-Saxons 73, 109
animism 14
ants 78
Arabian Nights 68
Aristaeus 85
Aristophanes, *The Birds* 11, 21, 98, 99
Aristotle 95
Armstrong, E. A. 61
Ascoli Piceno 27
Aubrey, John 39, 68
Augurs, College of 45–9
Augustine, Saint 100
auspices 47–9
Australia, aboriginal tribes 15

Babylon 9, 16, 18, 65
Bede 100
bee-eater 71
bees 83–7
bee-wolf 83
bestiaries 95–7
birds
  in divination, 44, 45
  as gods, 12
Blake, William 106

Boudicca 39
Brant, Sebastian 96

Camerarius 97
Carthage 25
Cats, Jacob 96
Celeus 79, 80, 85, 86
Chaucer, G. 88
Christianity, Christ 59, 95, 100, 102, 104, 105
Cicero 46, 47
Circe 38
Cnut, King 102
Coleridge, S. T. 106, 107
Cook, A. B. 19
Corybantes, the 87
Crete 9, 16–19, 75, 85, 86, 99
Cronos 16, 18, 21, 32
Culpeper N., 69, 70
Curetes, the 17, 38, 87
Cybele 87

Demeter 79, 80
Devil, the 80, 96, 102
Dionysios of Halicarnassus 52, 54
divination 43–51
Dodona 52, 54
Donar 64, 65, 73, 75
dowsers 72
Drayton, Michael 88
Druids 39, 75

Egypt, Egyptians 85, 95, 103
Eleusis 79
emblems 95–7
Estonia 61
Etruscans 33, 46

Faunus 32–4, 42, 55, 102
festivals 81
Fontainebleau, Forest of 94
France 56–8, 62, 71, 104, 110
Francis, Saint 106
Frazer, J. G. 61, 71, 75
Frija 73

Gemini 108
Gerard, John 69
German legends 70, 73, 74, 84, 110
Gertrude
  in folklore 59
  as substitute for Freya, 60
God 80, 96
Goddess, Great or Earth Mother 16, 19, 99, 103
Goethe, J. W. von 105
Greece 9, 21, 22, 47, 64, 75, 85, 99
Greek
  gods, 85
  philosophers, 49
Green Man, the 103
Gregory, The Great 100
Grimm, J. 60, 61, 70
Gubbio 26, 27
Gutslaff 61

Harris, Rendal 61, 62, 65, 86
Harrison, J. 55
harvest 80, 81
Heber, Bishop 105
herbs 67–70
Heroditus 95
Homer 32

honey 83–7
Horace 44
horses 80
Horus 103
Hudson, W. H. 92, 108

Iguvium 26
Illyria 24
Indians, American 65, 105
Iran 78
Ishtar 99
Isis 103
Israelites 83
Italy 9, 57, 75, 99

Jerusalem 75
Jefferies, Richard 90, 91
John, of Guildford 88, 109
Jung, Carl 50, 51, 107
Jupiter 32, 34, 38, 64, 65

Kuhn, F. 73

Lawson, J. C. 21
lituus 45, 46, 48

Macleod, Fiona *see* Sharp, W.
magic 14
mana 14, 15, 21
Mars 21, 23, 26, 31, 35, 39, 42, 44, 52, 63, 66, 82, 98, 99, 108
Marvell, Andrew 89, 90
Mercury 39
Mesopotamia 78, 85, 99
millers 59
Minoan culture 99
Minos 18
Monterubbiano 27
Montgomery, James 60
moon, cycles of 81
moonwort 69, 70

116 – Index

Murray, Gilbert 98, 99

Nature, worship of 104–8
neolithic 24
Newton, Isaac 104
Numa, King 32–4
numen 14, 33

oaks 63, 64, 85, 86
oracles 52–5
Ovid 29, 33, 38
Owen, J. A. 91

pagan customs 102
Palestine 78
Pan 21, 42, 85, 108
Paulinus 39
peony 69
Physiologus, the 95
Piceni, Picentes, Picenum 23–7
Picinelli 96, 97
Piciformes 3
Picker, Picken 61
Picus:
    as god 9, 10, 32–4, 42, 66, 86
    as king 18, 30, 38, 45
    link with Zeus 9, 11, 18, 21, 32
    as bird 30, 31, 38
    as oracle 52–5
    as ploughman 21, 78–80
    as totem 21–4
Pilumnus, and Picumnus 38
Plutarch 28, 33, 34, 44
Plato 47
Pliny 49, 67
Polytechnos 19, 20
Poland 80
Psellus 18
Pomona 38
Praetor, Aelius Tubero 49

Red Indian tribes 15, 81
religion, defined 13, 14
Rhea 16, 17, 31
Rome, Romans 21, 28–31, 32, 33, 35,
    38, 39, 45–9, 64, 75, 83, 85, 100
    citizenship 25
Romulus and Remus 9, 29, 30–2, 38,
    46, 48
Rousseau, J. J. 105, 106

Sabines 23, 24, 32, 35, 75
sacred spring 23, 24
Salii 35, 46
Saturn 9, 21, 30–2, 83
Scandinavia 60, 61, 64, 70
Sextus Pompeius 31
Sharp, William 93–5
Sky God 82, 100
springwort 67–77
Stoics 49, 51, 107
Strabo, *Geography* 23, 24
Suidas 18
Swabia 71, 74

taboos 75
Tacitus 39
Tammuz 16, 99
telegraph poles 84
Themis 85
Theodore, Archbishop 102
Thetford, treasure 39
Thomson, James 105
Thor 60, 64
thunder 21, 61, 64, 65, 73
Tiora Matiene 52, 55
totemism 15, 21
treasure, in folklore 73–5
Triptolemus 79, 85

Umbria 26, 35

Venus 82, 108
Virgil 29, 85, 87
Virgin, the Black 103

Wales 60, 72, 110
weather 21
Wells, city of 92, 108
White, Gilbert 2, 90
Willett, W. 92, 93
Woden 102
wolf 31
woodpecker, black 8, 60
woodpecker, great spotted 5
Woodpecker, green
   and augury 44, 45, 48, 49
   and bees 83–7
   call 2, 7, 22
   the chase of 27
   and Druids 39, 41
   habits 1–9
   in literature 88–94
   local folk names 109–111
   and omens 22
   and oracles 21, 22, 52–5
   and ploughing 78–82
   as rain-bird 56–66
   and Romans 28, 42
   and springwort 67–77
   as totem 24
woodpecker, grey headed 8
woodpecker, Levaillants 8
Wordsworth, William 106

Zeus 9, 11, 16–21, 32, 44, 62–5, 85–7, 99